The Jamestown Adventure

Other Titles in the Real Voices, Real History ™ Series

My Folks Don't Want Me to Talk About Slavery
Personal Accounts of Slavery in North Carolina
Edited by Belinda Hurmence

Before Freedom, When I Just Can Remember
Personal Accounts of Slavery in South Carolina
Edited by Belinda Hurmence

We Lived in a Little Cabin in the Yard
Personal Accounts of Slavery in Virginia
Edited by Belinda Hurmence

Mighty Rough Times, I Tell You
Personal Accounts of Slavery in Tennessee
Edited by Andrea Sutcliffe

On Jordan's Stormy Banks
Personal Accounts of Slavery in Georgia
Edited by Andrew Waters

Prayin' to Be Set Free
Personal Accounts of Slavery in Mississippi
Edited by Andrew Waters

I Was Born in Slavery
Personal Accounts of Slavery in Texas
Edited by Andrew Waters

Cherokee Voices
Early Accounts of Cherokee Life in the East
Edited by Vicki Rozema

Voices from the Trail of Tears
edited by Vicki Rozema

Weren't No Good Times
Personal Accounts of Slavery in Alabama
Edited by Horace Randall Williams

Black Indian Slave Narratives
edited by Patrick Minges

The Jamestown Adventure

Accounts of the Virginia Colony, 1605 – 1614

Edited by Ed Southern

John F. Blair, Publisher   Winston-Salem, North Carolina

The paper in this book meets the guidelines
for permanence and durability of the Committee on
Production Guidelines for Book Longevity
of the Council on Library Resources.

DESIGN BY DEBRA LONG HAMPTON

COVER MAP

from John Smith's *The General History of Virginia, New England, and the Summer Isles,*
published in 1624

Library of Congress Cataloging-in-Publication Data

The Jamestown adventure : accounts of the Virginia colony, 1605-1614 / edited
by Ed Southern.
    p.   cm.   (Real voices, real history series)
  Includes bibliographical references.
  ISBN 0-89587-302-8 (alk. paper)
  1. Jamestown (Va.)—History. 2. Jamestown (Va.)—History—Sources. I.
Southern, Ed, 1972- II. Series.

  F234.J3J325 2004
  975.5'4251—dc22

2004016037

Printed in Canada

Table of Contents

Acknowledgments

Working on this project made me wish, for the first time ever, that I had stayed in graduate school, particularly during my early, clumsy attempts at research. I owe great thanks, therefore, to those who did their best to fill in the yawning gaps in my knowledge. John Kneebone was an invaluable and generous resource in alerting me to the breadth and the location of Jamestown materials available. Two previous Real Voices, Real History™ editors, Vicki Rozema and Patrick Minges, anticipated many of the questions I would ask and set an excellent example to follow. An enthusiastic amateur like myself could not produce a modest volume like this, of course, without the diligent and skilled scholarship of the real historians whose work will be cited throughout this text. Naturally, I am grateful to those among the Jamestown colonists who saw fit to record their experience, whatever their motivation; while the accounts are testaments to the human will to endure, the fact that the accounts exist at all is a testament to the equally strong human will to leave a story behind.

I have the great good fortune of living in the same town as my alma mater, Wake Forest University, in whose Z. Smith Reynolds Library I was able to find first editions of most of the narratives used in this volume. Any editor can tell you the value of primary source materials, as opposed to later copies. As a book lover, though, access to four-hundred-year-old books, the actual physical texts that, however unlikely, could have been read by Shakespeare or John Donne, is an unrivalled thrill. I owe more thanks than I can express to rare books librarian Sharon Snow and her staff, whose support and hospitality never waned, no matter how many times I asked them to lug out all four massive volumes of *Purchas his Pilgrimes*.

Finally, I thank those who offered their support and encouragement. My co-workers at John F. Blair, Publisher, were enthusiastic about this project from the first mention. Carolyn Sakowski, Anne Waters, Steve Kirk, Kim Byerly, Sue Clark, Margaret Couch, Debbie Hampton, Dr. Heath Simpson, and Jackie Whitman were always willing to lend an ear or a good word. Ed Wilson and Susan Faust at Wake Forest are still as supportive as they were when I was a teen-aged undergrad, but have become better friends. My parents, Lynn Southern and Bob and Suzette Southern, and my siblings, Anna, Drew, and Jamie, were more excited about this book than I was, and my children, Corbyn and Molly, were gratifyingly curious. And for her patience, understanding, and strength, I owe the most thanks, always and above all, to Courtney.

Introduction

"And indeed nothing is easier for a man who has, as the phrase goes, 'followed the sea' with reverence and affection, than to evoke the great spirit of the past upon the lower reaches of the Thames. The tidal current runs to and fro in its unceasing service, crowded with memories of men and ships it had borne to the rest of home or to the battles of the sea . . . Hunters of gold or pursuers of fame, they all had gone out on that stream, bearing the sword, and often the torch, messengers of the might within the land, bearers of a spark from the sacred fire. What greatness had not floated on the ebb of that river into the mystery of an unknown earth! . . .The dreams of men, the seed of commonwealths, the germs of empires."

- Joseph Conrad, *Heart of Darkness*

In December 1606, three ships—the *Susan Constant*, the *Godspeed*, and the *Discovery*—sailed from London into the Thames reach described by Conrad. The small fleet carried 144 passengers and crew, each of them, to one degree or another, an employee of the Virginia Company of London, and each of them bound for a land that had already claimed more than its share of English lives.

In May of the following year, little more than 100 men would disembark to settle on a small peninsula in a river they called the King's, or, more personally, the James. Eight months later, only 38 men were still alive in the fort they had named Jamestown.[1]

Jamestown is well known as the first permanent English settlement in the New World; largely unknown is how fragile that permanence was—how close the colony came to failure, and in how many ways. Most Americans have a general awareness of the dangers faced on any frontier, but not the particular hardships that confronted the Jamestown colonists—starvation, disease, conspiracy, incompetent leaders, and, of course, intermittent war with the neighboring Native Americans. The colonists even packed up and left, once, only to meet their relief in the mouth of the Chesapeake Bay.

The Jamestown Adventure: Accounts of the Virginia Colony, 1605–1614 is part of the Real Voices, Real History™ series released by John F. Blair, Publisher. The titles in this series are concise, accessible presentations of first-hand accounts of some of the most challenging episodes in American history, such as slavery or the Cherokee removal. This volume collects contemporary accounts of the first successful colony in what would become the first thirteen United States. The earliest text dates from 1605, two years before the first landing; the last describes events up to 1614, when the marriage of Pocahontas and John Rolfe secured a brief measure of peace for the beleaguered colony. Most of the accounts were written by the colonists themselves; others reflect the perceptions and expectations of investors and observers back in

England, while two reveal the keen and hostile interest taken in the colony by England's chief rival, Spain. Several of them were written for widespread publication; others were either private letters or reports meant only for certain audiences. These narratives take the reader from the London stage to Powhatan's lodge, from the halls of royal power to the derelict hovels of the Starving Time. They speak of unimaginable suffering, cruelty, hope, and perseverance. They show the modern reader what an adventure the founding of English America was—the desperate battles and fraught negotiations with Powhatan and his warriors, the political intrigues in Europe and Virginia, the shipwreck that inspired a literary masterpiece, the captures and escapes, the discoveries that thrilled the colonists, the discoveries that broke their hearts.

The English in America

Those who invested their money in Virginia were called, in fact, adventurers; those who invested themselves in the new colony were called "adventurers in person." The Virginia Company of London was the latest in a century's worth of English attempts at colonization. Only five years after Columbus's first voyage, Henry VII sent John Cabot (born Giovanni Caboto in Genoa) across the Atlantic. Cabot "discovered" Cape Breton and Newfoundland, whose cod would bring English fishermen back for centuries and would save the Jamestown colony at least once. But the reign of Henry VIII would see only sporadic attempts to found colonies, all unsuccessful, some laughably so. England would not commit whole-heartedly to the sea until the ascension of Elizabeth I in 1558. While her astrologer John Dee wrote that English claims on lands beyond the sea could be traced back to

King Arthur, and her "sea dogs" explored the Arctic, harried the Spanish, and circled the globe, her sometime favorite Walter Raleigh tried time and again to gain a lasting English foothold on the American continent.

Raleigh's first expedition, in 1584, reconnoitered the coast of what is now North Carolina. His second, sent the following year, included a sort of "scientific research team" in the form of naturalist Thomas Hariot and artist John White, and left behind a garrison on Roanoke Island.[2] The garrison's commander, Ralph Lane, and his soldiers completely botched the heretofore friendly relations with the nearby Native Americans, and came close to starving, before Sir Francis Drake happened to stop by and was persuaded to carry the survivors back to England. Raleigh's third expedition, in 1587, was a serious attempt to found a thriving, growing English colony. Led by White, the group was comprised, not of soldiers, but of artisans, laborers, and families such as Ananias and Eleanor Dare, whose daughter Virginia would be the first English child born in America, and who would disappear as completely as the rest of this Lost Colony.

The story of the Lost Colony deserves more attention than can be paid to it here; in short, the situation at Roanoke was quickly recognized as untenable, and White returned to England to beg for help. Court politics and the threat of the Spanish Armada in 1588 delayed White's return until 1590, by which time the Roanoke settlement had been abandoned and the colonists had disappeared. The question—and the threat—of the Lost Colony's fate was to hang over Jamestown throughout the colony's early years, and will be brought up in several of the accounts in this book.

The death of Elizabeth in 1603 brought James I to the English throne. Far more respectful to the Spanish than Good Queen Bess had been, James had little sympathy for Raleigh's ambitions for an American base, and less for Raleigh himself. Within a year of taking office James had Raleigh tried on charges of high treason, in part to appease King Philip III of Spain. Raleigh was imprisoned in the Tower of London, and all the licenses and patents granted to him by Elizabeth—including the patent to Virginia—were revoked. In 1606 a group of investors—including many who had helped try and convict Raleigh—formed the Virginia Company to claim his abandoned interests in the New World.[3]

The royal charter of the Virginia Company divided it into two branches, one in Plymouth and one in London. They were to each establish a colony or outpost in North America, at least 100 miles apart from the other. The Virginia Company of Plymouth, in the summer of 1607, founded a colony called Fort Saint George on the Kennebec River in what is now Maine. Its major investor was lord chief justice John Popham, who had passed judgment at the trial of Raleigh; he died nine days after his colonists had set sail. After living through one Maine winter, the colonists decided to return to England, and Fort Saint George was abandoned for good after a little more than a year.

The Virginia Company of London, meanwhile, fitted out the three ships mentioned at the beginning of this introduction. To captain them they hired Christopher Newport, one of the last of the Elizabethan sea dogs that had bested the Spanish Armada and staked an English claim to the New World; Newport had, in fact, lost an arm in 1590, fighting the Spanish in the Caribbean. Under his command, at sea at least, were such men as Edward Maria Wingfield, an original investor in the Virginia Company; George Percy, the younger brother of the Earl of Northumberland; and an aggressive soldier named John Smith, who was accused of mutiny before the ships even crossed the Atlantic, and spent most of the voyage shackled and confined.

Once they landed, the adventurers were led by a seven-member council. The councilors had already been chosen by the Virginia Company, but their names were written in sealed orders that were not to be opened until the ships were within sight of their destination, the Chesapeake Bay.

The Jamestown Narratives

None of the accounts presented here can be taken at face value. Ivor Noel Hume, the former director of archaeology at Colonial Williamsburg, and one of the most compelling historians of the early colonies, says that "wide discrepancies among relatively contemporary accounts of the same incident demonstrate that any attempt to summarize events occurring 400 years ago is akin to skating in lead boots on melting ice."[4] Almost all of the Jamestown accounts went through the hands of at least one editor; in most cases, that editor was Samuel Purchas, a Cambridge-educated clergyman who acquired a vast library of exploration narratives that he published in a massive, four-volume work called *Purchas his Pilgrimes*. Purchas was a less-than-meticulous editor, but the publication of *Purchas his Pilgrimes* preserved accounts that might otherwise have been lost.

Each chronicler had a personal agenda, a hidden motive, an axe to grind. The chroniclers in the employ of the Virginia Company, for instance, were sworn to report only what was approved by the council in London; in other words, whatever would aid the colony's profitability. The chroniclers were also hampered by attitudes that they themselves would never have recognized as deficiencies. The galling arrogance towards the

Native Americans will not surprise most readers, but the schizophrenic view taken by many of the Jamestown chroniclers—who mingle appreciation and offhand condemnation with bewildering frequency—seems a harbinger of the "noble savage" ambivalence that still appears in perceptions of Native Americans. The similar mingling of cold-blooded, profit-driven pragmatism with sincere piety can also jar modern readers in ways that would not have occurred to most seventeenth century Europeans.

Readers will also be aware of whose stories are not being told at all. The tribes surrounding Jamestown left no written record of their own, and Virginia, at least at this early date, had no English equivalent to the Spanish Bartolome de las Casas, the Catholic priest who championed South and Central American natives and recorded their versions of the Spanish conquest. The "poorer sort" of Englishmen, with a few exceptions, had no chance to tell their side of the Virginia story, either. Except perhaps for the boy Henry Spelman, and for Smith, a professional soldier whose father was a smallholding farmer, the authors of these Jamestown narratives considered themselves gentlemen at the very least, and a few were much higher than that on the social scale. The historical record of Jamestown's early years lacks the perspectives, and often even the names, of the common laborers, sailors, and soldiers who kept the colony running.

Even with these limitations in mind, the Jamestown narratives reveal much about the nature of the colony—its aims and expectations, its hardships and quality of life. Personalities shine through the most self-serving accounts and the most opaque language. Those seeking the sturdy pioneers and noble heroes of American myth should look elsewhere. True heroes are hard to find in Jamestown; but then, so are unmitigated villains.

John Smith, to use the most famous example, may not have been the kind of guy usually Disneyfied: he was stubborn, vainglorious, ruthless, and spiteful. He was also forceful, brave, and quick-witted; when the colony's other leaders were plotting and complaining, Smith of his own initiative sought trade with the neighboring Indians, and arguably kept the colony alive, almost single-handedly, through its first two years.

The Language of the Narratives

Seventeenth-century English, unless written by a master, can seem haphazard, convoluted, and ungrammatical to twenty-first-century readers. The Jamestown narratives, in their original form, are no exception. Most of the writers were well-educated by any standard, but readers should keep in mind that more than a century would pass between the founding of Jamestown and the publication of Samuel Johnson's dictionary. Authors might spell a word, including a proper name, two or three different ways—even the same author, even in the same sentence.

To eliminate unnecessary difficulties, I have standardized spelling to comply with modern usage. For personal and place names, I have used either the version that is now commonly accepted—Jamestown rather than James Towne, Smith rather than Smythe—or the version most commonly used by the Virginia colonists. For Native American proper names, I have usually deferred to the spelling used by one or more of my secondary sources, although if a proper name is mentioned only once, I have left the word as the chronicler spelled it. Archaic or technical terms unfamiliar to general readers are followed by definitions set apart in brackets.

I have allowed myself to modernize punctuation in order to

make the narratives more accessible; however, I have not altered the sentence structures and phrasings. I wanted to make sure the narratives still sounded like seventeenth-century stories. The Jamestown chroniclers were contemporaries—and in the case of William Strachey, a friend—of some of the greatest craftsmen of the English language— Ben Jonson, John Donne, the translators of the King James Bible, and, of course, William Shakespeare. Breaking news from Jamestown inspired and fascinated these writers. Jonson collaborated on the 1605 play *Eastward Hoe*, an excerpt of which is included here, and later wrote a court masque that was performed before Rebecca Rolfe, nee Pocahontas. Most scholars now think it likely that Shakespeare saw a copy of Strachey's *A True Reportory . . .* , and that Strachey's story of shipwreck on Bermuda gave Shakespeare the idea that would become *The Tempest*.

If a writer comparable to Jonson, Donne, or Shakespeare came to Jamestown, their thoughts and work have not survived; quite likely, the writer himself did not survive, in a colony whose mortality rate hovered around 80 per cent until the middle of the seventeenth century. Still, the writers whose work is assembled here had magnificent stories to tell, and most of them told their stories with skill and power. *The Jamestown Adventure* is not a comprehensive history of early Virginia, nor is it a comprehensive collection of first-hand accounts of Jamestown. Rather, this book is an attempt to take modern readers past the myths and generalizations about the founding colonists, and introduce them to the individuals who manned a small outpost on the far side of the world.

The actor and author Simon Callow, in a 2004 review for the British newspaper *The Guardian*, wrote that "it scarcely needs underlining that knowing what America is, where it comes from and how it might act has never been more important." I hope that *The Jamestown Adventure* is, first and foremost, an exciting read; but I also hope that it makes a small contribution to our knowledge of where America comes from. If the United States began at Jamestown, so did the nation's ongoing wrestling match between its ideals and its reality. Notions of democracy, of the chance to build a better life, and of the sublime perception of wilderness, entered this continent through a small peninsula in the James River. So did the corrupting power of corporate greed, the slavery of Africans, and the genocidal wars against the Native Americans. If our history is to be at all helpful to our future, it needs to be known and understood on as personal a level as possible.

NOTES

1. Wertenbaker, Thomas Jefferson, *Virginia Under the Stuarts, 1607-1688* (Princeton: Princeton University Press, 1914), 1.

2. Hume, Ivor Noel, *The Virginia Adventure: Roanoke to James Towne, An Archaeological and Historical Odyssey* (Charlottesville: University Press of Virginia, 1994), 29.

3. Miller, Lee, *Roanoke: Solving the Mystery of the Lost Colony* (New York: Arcade Publishing, 2001), 208-9, 212.

4. Hume, *The Virginia Adventure*, 110.

PART I

"Come, boys, Virginia longs"

1605-1606

A Colonial Con Job

From *Eastward Hoe*,
by George Chapman, Ben Jonson, and John Marston[1]

> *Eastward Hoe was performed by the Children of Her
> Majesty's Revels (one of whose shareholders would later
> be secretary of the Jamestown colony) at the Blackfriars
> theater in London sometime after Christmas 1604. The
> play's ridicule of Scots (not a good idea, since James I of
> England had been James VI of Scotland first) earned the
> Roman Catholic Jonson a second stay in prison, which
> evidently helped him see the true light of the Anglican
> Church.[2] The plot of the comedy borrows heavily from
> the story of the Prodigal Son, but our concern is with
> the second scene of the third act, in which a blowhard
> "Captain" seduces two Londoners with fantastic stories
> of the fabulous riches of Virginia.[3]*
>
> *The English had yet to establish a successful foothold
> in America. The aggressive expansionism of Elizabeth
> had been replaced with the cautious pacifism of James,
> and Virginia expeditions were becoming something of a
> joke. That includes the expedition now known as the Lost*

Colony, to which the play refers, albeit by the wrong date. Details aside, the mention shows that the mystery of the colonists' fate occupied a place in the English consciousness; they were lost, but not forgotten.

From Act 3, Scene 2

Enter Seagull, Spendall, and Scapthrift in the Tavern with a Drawer.

Seagull: Come Drawer, pierce your neatest hogshead, and let's have cheer, not fit for your Billingsgate Tavern, but for our Virginia Colonel; he will be here instantly.

Drawer: You shall have all things fit, sir; please you have any more wine?

Spendall: More wine, slave? Whether we drink it or no, spill it, and draw more.

Scapthrift: Fill all the pots in your house with all sorts of liquor, and let 'em wait on us here like soldiers in their pewter coats; and though we do not employ them now, yet we will maintain 'em, till we do.

Drawer: Said like an honorable captain; you shall have all you can command, sir.

Exit Drawer.

Seagull: Come, boys, Virginia longs till we share the rest of her maidenhead.

Spendall: Why, is she inhabited already with any English?

Seagull: A whole country of English is there, man, bred of those that were left there in '79. They have married with the Indians, and make 'em bring forth as beautiful faces as any we have in England. And therefore the Indians are so in love with 'em, that all the treasure they have, they lay at their feet.

Scapthrift: But is there such treasure there, Captain, as I have heard?

Seagull: I tell thee, gold is more plentiful there than copper is with us. And for as much red copper as I can bring, I'll have thrice the weight in gold. Why, man, all their dripping pans, and their chamber pots are pure gold; and all the chains, with which they chain up their streets, are massie [massive] gold. All the prisoners they take are fettered in gold; and for rubies and diamonds, they go forth on holidays and gather 'em by the seashore, to hang on their children's coats, and stick in their caps, as commonly as our children wear saffron-gilt brooches, and groats [kernels] with holes in 'em.

Scapthrift: And is it a pleasant country withall?

Seagull: As ever the sun shine on, temperate and full of all sorts of excellent viands. Wild boar is as common there as our tamest bacon is here; venison, as mutton. And then you shall live freely there, without sergeants, or courtiers, or lawyers, or intelligencers … Then for your means to advancement, there, it is simple, and not preposterously mixed: you may be an alderman there, and never be scavenger; you may be a nobleman, and never be a slave; you may come to preferment enough, and never be a pander; to riches and fortune enough, and have never the more villainy, nor the less wit.

Spendall: Gods me! And how far is it thether?

Seagull: Some six weeks' sail, no more, with any indifferent good wind. And if I get to any part of the coast of Africa, I'll sail thether with any wind. Or when I come to Cape Finister, there's a fortnight wind continually wafts us till we come at Virginia.[4]

NOTES

1. Chapman, George, Ben Jonson, and John Marston, *Eastward Hoe*, edited with an introduction, glossary, and notes by Julia Hamlet Harris, (New Haven: Yale University Press, 1926), 44-47.

2. Palmer, Alan and Veronica. *Who's Who in Shakespeare's England* (New York: St. Martin's Press, 1999), 136.

3. Chapman, George, Ben Jonson, and John Marston, ix.

4. Cape Finister, at the northwest corner of the Iberian peninsula, was a common landmark for northern European ships setting off across the Atlantic. It marked the general point at which the ships changed course to the west.

Instructions for the First Colonists

From
"Instructions given by way of advice by us whom it hath pleased the King's Majesty to appoint of the council for the intended voyage to Virginia, to be observed by those captains and company which are sent at this present to plant there."[1]

The original royal charter of the Virginia Company, granted in 1606, called for a London-based council to manage the colony through a second council based in Virginia. The council in London, whose members were the company's leading investors and included some of the most powerful men in the kingdom, answered directly to the king's Privy Council.[2] Relations between the Virginia council and the king were strained at the best of times. The youth of James I had been marked by violent death, including the execution of his mother Mary, Queen of Scots, by his predecessor Elizabeth. He had no enthusiasm for provoking the still-powerful Spanish; one of his first acts as king was to formalize a peace with Philip III of Spain. This pacifism, combined with a lack of interest in sea power and a visceral aversion to tobacco, made the king suspicious of the whole Virginia venture, particularly its roots in the "remnants of Elizabeth's old order."[3]

One of those remnants was the clergyman, scholar, and unflagging propagandist Richard Hakluyt. Though he never left the island himself, Hakluyt was an early and devoted proponent of England's exploration of and claims to foreign lands. From his student days he read everything he could (which was a lot, since he could read six languages) about the Age of Discovery in which he found himself. Later he would compile and edit these accounts for publication in a series of books, which are credited with "doing most to put England in an empire-building vein" and made the non-seafaring Hakluyt the leading authority on foreign lands.[4]

Hakluyt was one of the original Virginia Company shareholders; the council's instructions undoubtedly drew heavily from his accumulated knowledge. These instructions cover every possible contingency, from the placement and governance of the new town, to relations with the Indians, to the most likely place to find the long-sought route to the South Seas. The colonists would discover how well these instructions fit the realities of Virginia.

As we doubt not but you will have especial care to observe the ordinances sent down by the King's Majesty and delivered unto you under the privy seal, so for your better directions upon your first landing we have thought good to recommend unto your care these instructions and articles following.

When it shall please God to send you on the coast of Virginia, you shall do your best endeavor to find out a safe port in the entrance of some navigable river making choice of such a one as runneth farthest into the land, and if you happen to discover divers portable rivers, and amongst them any one that have two main branches, if the difference be not great make choice of that which bendeth most toward the northwest for that way you shall soonest find the other sea.

When you have made choice of the river on which you mean to settle be not hasty in landing your victuals and munitions, but first let Captain Newport discover how far that river may be found navigable that you make election of the strongest, most wholesome and fertile place for if you make many removes, besides the loss of time, you shall greatly spoil your victuals and your casks, and with great pain transport it in small boats.

But if you choose your place so far up as a bark of 50 tons will float then you may lay all your provisions ashore with ease, and the better receive the trade of all the countries about you in the land, and such a place you may perchance find a hundred miles from the river's mouth, and the further up the better, for if you sit down near the entrance, except it be in some island that is strong by nature, an enemy that may approach you on even ground may easily pull you out, and if he be driven to seek you a hundred miles the land in boats you shall from both sides of the river where it is narrowest so beat them with your muskets as they shall never be able to prevail against you.

And to the end that you be not surprised . . . you shall do

well to make this double provision: first erect a little store at the mouth of the river that may lodge some ten men, with whom you shall leave a light boat, that when any fleet shall be in sight they may come with speed to give you warning. Secondly you must in no case suffer any of the native people of the country to inhabit between you and the sea coast, for you cannot carry yourselves so towards them but they will grow discontented with your habitation, and be ready to guide and assist any nation that shall come to invade you, and if you neglect this you neglect your safety.

When you have discovered as far up the river as you mean to plant yourselves and landed your victuals and munitions . . . You shall do well to divide your six score men into three parts, whereof one party of them you may appoint to fortify and build of which your first work must be your storehouse for victual; the other you may employ in preparing your ground and sowing your corn and roots; the other ten of these forty you must leave as sentinel at the haven's mouth. The other forty you may employ for two months in discovery of the river above you, and on the country about you, which charge Captain Newport and Captain Gosnold may undertake of these forty discoverers; when they do espy any high lands or hills Captain Gosnold may take 20 of the company to cross over the lands and carrying a half dozen pickaxes to try if they can find any minerals. The other twenty may go on by river, and pitch up boughs upon the bank's side by which the other boats shall follow them by the same turnings. You may also take with them a wherry [a light rowboat used for one person] such as is used here in the Thames, by which you may send back to the president for supply of munition or any other want that you may not be driven to return for every small defect.

You must observe if you can whether the river on which you plant doth spring out of mountains or out of lakes; if it be out of any lake the passage to the other sea will be the more easy. It is like enough that out of the same lake you shall find some spring which run the contrary way toward the east India sea . . .

In all your passages you must have great care not to offend the naturals if you can eschew it, and employ some few of your company to trade with them for corn and all other lasting victuals if you have any; and this you must do before that they perceive that you mean to plant among them, for not being sure how your own seed corn will prosper the first year, to avoid the danger of famine, use and endeavor to store yourselves of the country corn.

Your discoverers that passes over lands with hired guides, must look well to them that they slip not from them, and for more assurance, let them take a compass with them, and write down how far they go upon every point of the compass, for that country having no way nor path, if that your guides run from you in the great woods or desert, you shall hardly ever find a passage back.

And how weary so ever your soldiers be, let them never trust the country people with the carriage of their weapons, for if they run from you with your shot which they only fear, they will easily kill them all with their arrows. And whensoever any of you shoots before them, be sure that they be chosen out of your best marksmen, for if they see your learners miss what they aim at, they will think the weapon not so terrible and thereby will be bold to assault you.

Above all things do not advertise the killing of any of your men, that the country people may know it; if they perceive that they are but common men, and that with the loss of many of theirs, they may diminish any part of yours, they will make many adventures upon you. If the country be populous, you shall do well also not to let them see or know of your sick men, if you have any, which may also encourage them to many enterprises. You must take especial care that you choose a seat for habitation that shall not be overburthened with woods near your town for all the men you have shall not be able to cleanse twenty acres a year, besides that it may serve for a covert for your enemies round about.

Neither must you plant in a low or moist place because it will prove unhealthful. You shall judge of the good air by the people, for some part of that coast where the lands are low have their people blear eyed and with swollen bellies and legs, but if the naturals be strong and clean made it is a true sign of a wholesome soil.

You must take order to draw up the pinnace [a light sailing ship] that is left with you under the fort, and take her sails and anchors ashore, all but a small ketch to ride by, lest some ill disposed persons slip away with her.

You must take care that your mariners that go for wages do not mar your trade, for those that mind not to inhabit, for a little game will debase the estimation of exchange, and hinder the trade forever after, and therefore you shall [not] admit or suffer any person whatsoever, other than such as shall be appointed by the president and council there, to buy any merchandise or other things whatsoever. . . .

You shall do well to send a perfect relation by Captain Newport of all that is done, what height you are seated, how far into the land, what commodities you find, what soil, woods and their several kinds, and so of all other things else to advertise particularly; and to suffer no man to return but by passport from the president and council, nor to write any letter of anything that may discourage others.

Lastly and chiefly the way to prosper and achieve good success is to make yourselves all of one mind for the good of your country and your own, and to serve and fear God the Giver of all Goodness, for every plantation which our Heavenly Father hath not planted shall be rooted out.

NOTES

1.Neill, Edwards S., *History of the Virginia Company of London* (Albany: Joel Munsell, 1869), 8-14.

2.Wertenbaker, Thomas Jefferson, *Virginia Under the Stuarts*, 1607-1688 (Princeton: Princeton University Press, 1914), 2.

3.Hume, Ivor Noel, *The Virginia Adventure: Roanoke to James Towne, An Archaeological and Historical Odyssey* (Charlottesville: University Press of Virginia, 1994), 112.

4.Ibid., 28.

PART II

"This New Discovered Virginia"

1607-1608

The Arrival

Letter of the Council in Virginia to the Council in England, June 22, 1607[1]

When the Susan Constant, Godspeed, *and* Discovery *were within a day's sail of the Chesapeake Bay, Captain Christopher Newport opened the sealed orders from the Virginia Company and read the names of those who would run the new colony. The names had been kept secret throughout the voyage in order, if not to reduce the chances of jealousy and strife, then at least to postpone them until the colonists had reached Virginia.*[2]

Edward Maria Wingfield, one of the company's earliest investors, and one of the few investors to make the voyage himself, was elected president. The Godspeed's *Captain Bartholomew Gosnold and the* Discovery's *John Ratcliffe, both of whom intended to stay in Virginia, were also named to the council, as were George Kendall and John Martin. The sixth councilor was, rather awkwardly, the imprisoned John Smith, who barely had been out of sight of Europe before Newport accused him of mutinous plotting. Newport was a councilor for as long as he stayed in Virginia, which turned out to be about six weeks. Having consulted with Wingfield, and believing the colony to be sufficiently well supplied to last until his return that winter, Newport set sail in June, carrying this letter with him.*

Some of the claims made in this letter, especially the claim to be "fortified well," have been disputed not only by modern historians but by subsequent accounts of the Jamestown colony. The claim that they settled 80 miles up the James River can be disputed by a quick look at a map of Virginia, which shows Jamestown (which is now on an island rather than a peninsula) to be about 30 miles from the mouth of the James. The pressure to tell the stockholders what they wanted to hear would be a continuing worry in Jamestown.

We acknowledge ourselves accomptable for our time here spent, were it but to give you satisfaction of our industries and affections to this most honorable action, and the better to quicken those good spirits which have already bestowed themselves here, and to put life into such dead understandings or beliefs that must first see and feel the womb of our labor and this land before they will entertain any good hope of us or of the land.

Within less than seven weeks, we are fortified well against the Indians. We have sown good store of wheat—we have sent you a taste of clapboard—we have built some houses—we have spared some hands to a discovery, and still as God shall enable us with strength we will better and better our proceedings.

Our easiest and richest commodity, being sassafras roots, were gathered up by the sailors with loss and spoil of many of our tools and with drawing of our men from our labor to their uses against our knowledge to our prejudice, we earnestly entreat you (and do trust) that you take such order as we be not in this thus defrauded, since they be all our waged men, yet do we wish that they be reasonably dealt withall so as all the loss neither fall on us nor them. I believe they have thereof two tons at the least which if they scatter abroad at their pleasure will pull down our price for a long time; this we leave to your wisdoms . . .

We are set down 80 miles within a river, for breadth, sweetness of water, length navigable up into the country, deep and bold channel so stored with sturgeon and other sweet fish as no man's fortune hath ever possessed the like. And as we think if more may be wished in a river it will be found. The soil is most fruitful, laden with good oak, ash, walnut tree, poplar, pine, sweetwoods, cedar, and others yet without names that yield gums pleasant as frankincense, and experienced amongst us for great virtue in healing green wounds and aches. We entreat your succors for our seconds with all expedition, lest that all-devouring Spaniard lay his ravenous hands upon these gold-showing mountains, which if we be so enabled he shall never dare to think on.[3]

. . . This note doth make known where our necessities do most strike us, we beseech your present relief accordingly, otherwise to our greatest and last griefs, we shall against our wills not will that which we most willingly would.

Captain Newport hath seen all and knoweth all, he can fully satisfy your further expectations, and ease you of our tedious

"Never were Englishmen . . . in more misery"

"Observations gathered out of a Discourse of the Plantation of the Southern Colony in Virginia by the English, 1608. Written by that Honorable Gentleman, Master George Percy."[1]

George Percy was the younger brother of Henry Percy, the ninth Earl of Northumberland, a noble title with Shakespearean resonance that could be traced back for centuries. As the eighth son, however, George had no prospects commensurate with his lineage; worse, his whole family had fallen out of favor with James I because of his brother's suspected complicity in the Gunpowder Plot (for more information about the Gunpowder Plot, see "A Spy in the Palace"). Educated at Oxford and at Middle Temple in London, Percy—like many Jamestown colonists—had acquired military experience fighting with the Dutch in their rebellion against Spain. He was twenty-seven years old when he sailed for Virginia, an almost exact contemporary of his social opposite John Smith.

Upon landing, Captain Christopher Newport, following the council's instructions, divided the colonists into three groups: builders to start constructing the fort, storehouse, and lodgings; agriculturalists to clear ground and plant foodstuffs and commercial crops; and explorers to travel further up the James River in search of neighboring tribes, possible clues to the fate of the Lost Colony, and, most importantly, valuable commodities, preferably the yellow-colored, rock-like kind. Like any decent, gold-hungry gentleman, Percy and the colony's other leaders signed up to be explorers, leaving minor considerations such as food and shelter to the commoners.

Percy, along with John Smith, was one of early Virginia's most careful and compelling chroniclers; his "Discourse of the Plantation of the Southern Colony in Virginia" is the most detailed account of life in the colony's first year, and was later collected by Purchas (see the introduction) and published as "Observations gathered out of a Discourse" in Purchas His Pilgrim. Percy describes the first, usually friendly encounters with the neighboring Native American tribes, as well as their customs that Percy was able to observe. He also describes vividly the abundant land and wildlife the English found in Virginia, and the misery they faced from dwindling food supplies and rampant illness. Percy's account ends with a roll call of the dead.

On Saturday, the twentieth of December, in the year 1606, the fleet fell from London, and the fifth of January we anchored in the Downs [in the English Channel]. But the winds continued contrary for so long that we were forced to stay there some time, where we suffered great storms, but by the skillfulness of the Captain we suffered no great loss or danger. . . .

The six and twentieth of April, about four o'clock in the morning, we descried the land of Virginia. The same day we entered into the bay of Chesapeake directly, without any let or hindrance. There we landed, and discovered a little way, but we could find nothing worth the speaking of, but fair meadows and goodly tall trees, with such fresh waters running through the woods, as I was almost ravished at the first sight thereof.

At night, when we were going aboard, there came the savages creeping on all fours, from the hills like bears, with their bows in their mouths, charged us very desperately in the faces, hurt Captain Gabriel Archer in both his hands, and a sailor in two places of the body very dangerous. After they had spent their arrows, and felt the sharpness of our shot, they retired into the woods with a great noise, and so left us.

The seven and twentieth day we began to build up our shallop [a vessel used for sailing or rowing in shallow water]. The gentlemen and soldiers marched eight miles up into the land. We could not see a savage in all that march. We came to a place where they had made a great fire, and had been newly roasting oysters; when they perceived our coming, they fled away to the mountains, and left many of the oysters in the fire. We ate some of the oysters, which were very large and delicate in taste.

The eighteenth day we launched our shallop. The Captain

[Newport] and some gentlemen went in her, and discovered up the Bay. We found a river on the south side running into the main; we entered it and found it very shoaled water, not for any boats to swim. We went further into the Bay, and saw a plain plot of ground where we went on land, and found the place five miles in compass, without either bush or tree. We saw nothing there but a canoe, which was made out of the whole tree, which was five and forty foot long by the rule. Upon this plot of ground we got good store of mussels and oysters, which lay on the ground as thick as stones. We opened some, and found in many of them pearls. We marched some three or four miles further into the woods, where we saw great smokes of fire. We marched to those smokes and found that the savages had been there burning down the grass, as we thought either to make their plantation there, or else to give signs to bring their forces together, and so to give us battle. We passed through excellent ground full of flowers of divers kinds and colors, and as goodly trees as I have seen, as cedar, cypress, and other kinds. Going a little further we came into a little plat of ground full of fine and beautiful strawberries, four times bigger and better than ours in England. All this march we could neither see savage nor town. When it grew to be towards night we stood back to our ships. We sounded and found it shallow water for a great way, which put us out of all hopes for getting any higher with our ships, which rode at the mouth of the river. We rowed over to a point of land, where we found a channel, and sounded six, eight, ten, or twelve fathom, which put us in good comfort. Therefore we named that point of land Cape Comfort.

The nine and twentieth day we set up a cross at Chesapeake Bay, and named that place Cape Henry. Thirtieth day, we came with our ships to Cape Comfort, where we saw five savages running on the shore. Presently the Captain caused the shallop to be manned, so rowing to the shore, the Captain called to them in sign of friendship, but they were at first very timorsome, until they saw the Captain lay his hand on his heart. Upon that they laid down their bows and arrows, and came very boldly to us, making signs to come ashore to their town, which is called by the savages Kecoughtan [near modern Hampton]. We coasted to their town, rowing over a river running into the main, where these savages swarm over with their bows and arrows in their mouths.

When we came over to the other side, there was a many of other savages which directed us to their town, where we were entertained by them very kindly. When we came first a land they made a doleful noise, laying their faces to the ground, scratching the earth with their nails. We did think that they had been at their idolatry. When they had ended their ceremonies, they went into their houses and brought out mats and laid upon the ground. The chiefest of them sat all in a rank; the meanest sort brought us such dainties as they had, and of their bread, which they made of their maize or guinea wheat. They would not suffer us to eat unless we sat down, which we did on a mat right against them. After we were well satisfied they gave us of their tobacco, which they took in a pipe made artificially of earth as ours are, but far bigger, with the bowl fashioned together with a piece of fine copper. After they had feasted us, they showed us, in welcome, their manner of dancing, which was in this fashion: one of the savages standing in the midst singing, beating one hand against another, all the rest dancing about him, shouting, howling, and stamping against the ground, with many antic tricks and faces, making noise like so many wolves and devils. One thing of them I observed: when they were in their dance they kept stroke with their feet just one with another, but with their hands, heads, faces, and bodies, every one of them had a several gesture. So they continued for the space of half an hour. When they had ended their dance, the Captain gave them beads and other trifling jewels. They hang through their ears fowls' legs. They shave the right side of their heads with a shell; the left side they wear of an ell [about 45 inches] long tied up with an artificial knot, with a many of fowls' feathers sticking in it. They go altogether naked, but their privities are covered with beasts' skins beset commonly with little bones, or beasts' teeth. Some paint their bodies black, some red, with artificial knots of sundry lively colors, very beautiful and pleasing to the eye, in a braver fashion than they in the West Indies.

The fourth day of May, we came to the King or Werowance of Paspahegh, where they entertained us with much welcome. An old savage made a long oration, making a foul noise, uttering his speech with a vehement action, but we knew little what they meant. Whilst we were in company with the Paspaheghs, the Werowance of Rappahanna came from the other side of the river in his canoe. He seemed to take displeasure of our being with the Paspaheghs. He would fain have had us to come to his town; the Captain was unwilling, seeing that the day was so far spent. He returned back to his ships for that night.

The next day, being the fifth of May, the Werowance of Rappahanna sent a messenger to have us come to him. We entertained the said messenger, and gave him trifles which pleased him. We manned our shallop with muskets and targatiers [small shields] sufficiently; this said messenger guided us where our determination was to go. When we landed, the Werowance of Rappahanna came down to the water side with all his train, as goodly men as any I have seen of savages or

Christians. The Werowance coming before them playing on a flute made of a reed, with a crown of deer's hair colored red, in fashion of a rose, fastened about his knot of hair, and a great plate of copper on the other side of his head, with two long feathers in fashion of a pair of horns placed in the midst of his crown. His body was painted all with crimson, with a chain of beads about his neck, his face painted blue, besprinkled with silver ore as we thought, his ears all behung with bracelets of pearl, and in either ear a bird's claw through it, beset with fine copper or gold. He entertained us in so modest a proud fashion, as though he had been a prince of civil government, holding his countenance without laughter or any such ill behavior. He caused his mat to be spread on the ground, where he sat down with a great majesty, taking a pipe of tobacco, the rest of his company standing about him. After he had rested a while he rose, and made signs to us to come to his town. He went foremost, and all the rest of his people and ourselves followed him up a steep hill where his palace was settled. We passed through the woods in fine paths, having most pleasant springs which issued from the mountains. We also went through the goodliest cornfields that ever was seen in any country. When we came to Rappahanna's town, he entertained us in good humanity.

The eighth day of May we discovered up the river. We landed in the country of Appomattoca. At our landing, there came many stout and able savages to resist us with their bows and arrows, in a most warlike manner, with the swords at their backs beset with sharp stones, and pieces of iron able to cleave a man in sunder. Amongst the rest, one of the chiefest, standing before them crosslegged, with his arrow ready in his bow in one hand, and taking a pipe of tobacco in the other, with a bold uttering of his speech, demanded of us our being there, willing us to be gone. We made signs of peace, which they perceived in the end, and let us land in quietness.

The twelfth day we went back to our ships, and discovered a point of land, called Archer's Hope, which was sufficient, with a little labor, to defend ourselves against any enemy. The soil was good and fruitful, with excellent good timber. There are also great store of vines in bigness of a man's thigh, running up to the tops of the trees in great abundance. We also did see many squirrels, conies, rabbits, black birds with crimson wings, and divers other fowls and birds of divers and sundry colors . . . We found store of turkey nests and many eggs. If it had not been disliked, because the ship could not ride near the shore, we had settled there to all the colony's contentment.

The thirteenth day we came to our seating place in Paspahegh's country, some eight miles from the point of land, which I made mention before, where our ships do lie so near the shore that they are moored to the trees in six fathom water.

The fourteenth day we landed all our men which were set to work about the fortification, and others some to watch and ward as it was convenient. The first night of our landing, about midnight, there came some savages sallying close to our quarter. Presently there was an alarum given; upon that the savages ran away, and we not troubled anymore by them that night. Not long after, there came two savages that seemed to be commanders, bravely dressed, with crowns of colored hair upon their heads, which came as messengers from the Werowance of Paspahegh, telling us that their Werowance was coming and would be merry with us with a fat deer.

The eighteenth day, the Werowance of Paspahegh came himself to our quarter, with one hundred savages armed, which guarded him in a very warlike manner with bows and arrows, thinking at that time to execute their villainy. Paspahegh made great signs to us to lay our arms away. But we would not trust him so far. He, seeing he could not have convenient time to work his will, at length made signs that he would give us as much land as we would desire to take. As the savages were in a throng in the fort, one of them stole a hatchet from one of our company, which spied him doing the deed, whereupon he took it from him by force, and also struck him over the arm. Presently, another savage, seeing that, came fiercely at our man with a wooden sword, thinking to beat out his brains. The Werowance of Paspahegh saw us take to our arms, went suddenly away with all his company in great anger.

The nineteenth day, myself and three or four more, walking into the woods, by chance we espied a pathway. We were desirous to know whither it would bring us. We traced along some four miles, all the way as we went, having the pleasantest suckles, the ground all flowing over with fair flowers of sundry colors and kinds, as though it had been in any garden or orchard in England. There be many strawberries, and other fruits unknown. We saw the woods full of cedar and cypress trees, with other trees, which issue out sweet gums like to balsam. We kept on our way in this paradise; at length we came to a savage town, where we found but few people. They told us the rest were gone a-hunting with the Werowance of Paspahegh. We stayed there a while, and had of them strawberries, and other things. In the meantime one of the savages came running out of his house with a bow and arrows and ran mainly through the woods. Then I began to mistrust some villainy, that he went to call some company, and so betray us. We made all the haste away we could. One of the savages brought us on the way to the wood side, where there was a garden of tobacco, and other fruits and herbs. He gathered tobacco, and distributed to every one of us, so we departed.

The twentieth day the Werowance of Paspahegh sent forty of his men with a deer to our quarter, but they came more in villainy than any love they bare us. They fain would have lain in our fort all night, but we would not suffer them for fear of their treachery. One of our gentlemen, having a target which he trusted in, thinking it would bear out a slight shot, he set it up against a tree, willing one of the savages to shoot; who took from his back an arrow of an ell long, drew it strongly in his bow, shoots the target a foot through, or better, which was strange, being that a pistol could not pierce it. We, seeing the force of his bow, afterwards set him up a steel target; he shot again, and burst his arrow all to pieces. He presently pulled out another arrow, and bit it in his teeth, and seemed to be in a great rage, so he went away in great anger.

Their bows are made of tough hazel, their strings of leather, their arrows of canes or hazel, headed with very sharp stones, and are made artificially like a broad arrow. Other some of their arrows are headed with the ends of deer's horns, and are feathered very artificially.

At Port Cotage in our voyage up the river, we saw a savage boy about the age of ten years, which had a head of hair of a perfect yellow and a reasonable white skin, which is a miracle amongst all savages.[2]

This river which we have discovered is one of the famousest rivers that ever was found by any Christian. It ebbs and flows a hundred and threescore miles, where ships of great burden may harbor in safety. Wheresoever we landed upon this river we saw the goodliest woods as beech, oak, cedar, cypress, walnuts, sassafras and vines in great abundance, which hang in great clusters on many trees, and other trees unknown, and all the grounds bespread with many sweet and delicate flowers of divers colors and kinds. There are also many fruits as strawberries, mulberries, raspberries, and fruits unknown. There are many branches of this river, which run flowing through the woods with great plenty of fish of all kinds; as for sturgeon, all the world cannot be compared to it. In this country I have seen many great and large meadows, having excellent good pasture for any cattle. There is also great store of deer, both red and fallow. There are bears, foxes, otters, beavers, muskrats, and wild beasts unknown.

The four and twentieth day we set up a cross at the head of this river, naming it King's River, where we proclaimed James, King of England, to have the most right unto it. When we had finished and set up our cross, we shipped our men and made for James Fort. By the way we came to Powhatan's Town where the Captain went on shore, suffering none to go with him.[3] He presented the commander of this place with a hatchet, which he took joyfully, and was well pleased.

But yet the savages murmured at our planting in the country, whereupon this Werowance made answer again, very wisely of a savage, "Why should you be offended with them as long as they hurt you not, nor take anything away by force? They take but a little waste ground, which doth you nor any of us any good."

I saw bread made by their women, which do all their drudgery. The men take their pleasure in hunting and their wars, which they are in continually, one kingdom against another. . . .

There is notice to be taken to know married women from maids. The maids, you shall always see the fore part of their head and sides shaven close, the hinder part very long, which they tie in a plait hanging down to their hips. The married women wear their hair all of a length, and is tied of that fashion that the maids are. The womenkind in this country doth pounce and race their bodies, legs, thighs, arms, and faces with a sharp iron, which makes a stamp in curious knots, and draws the proportion of fowls, fish, or beasts, then with paintings of sundry lively colors, they rub it into the stamp, which will never be taken away, because it is dried into the flesh where it is seared.

The savages bear their years well, for when we were at Pamunkey, we saw a savage [who] by their report was above eight score years of age. His eyes were sunk into his head, having never a tooth in his mouth, his hair all gray with a reasonable big beard, which was as white as any snow. It is a miracle to see a savage have any hair on their faces; I never saw, read, nor heard, any have the like before. This savage was as lusty and went as fast as any of us, which was strange to behold.

The fifteenth day of June, we had built and finished our fort, which was triangle-wise, having three bulwarks at every corner like a half-moon, and four or five pieces of artillery mounted in them. We had made ourselves sufficiently strong for these savages. We had also sown most of our corn on two mountains. It sprang a man's height from the ground. This country is a fruitful soil, bearing many goodly and fruitful trees. . . .

Monday, the two and twentieth of June, in the morning Captain Newport in the *Admiral* departed from James Port for England. Captain Newport being gone for England, leaving us (one hundred and four persons) very bare and scanty of victuals, furthermore in wars and in danger of the savages. We hoped after a supply, which Captain Newport promised within twenty weeks. But if the beginners of this action do carefully further us, the country being so fruitful, it would be as great a profit to the realm of England, as the Indies to the King of Spain. If this river which we have found had been discovered in the time of war with Spain, it would have been a commodity to our realm, and a great annoyance to our enemies. The seven and twentieth of July the King of Rappahanna demanded a canoe, which was restored. [He] lifted up his hand to the sun, which they worship as their god, besides he laid his hand on his heart, that he would be our special friend. It is a general rule of these people when they swear by their god which is the sun, no Christian will keep their oath better upon this promise.

These people have a great reverence to the sun above all other things. At the rising and setting of the same, they sit down, lifting up their hands and eyes to the sun, making a round circle on the ground with dried tobacco. Then they begin to pray, making many devilish gestures with a hellish noise, foaming at the mouth, staring with their eyes, wagging their heads and hands in such a fashion and deformity as it was monstrous to behold.

The sixth of August there died John Asbie of the bloody flux. The ninth day died George Flowre of the swelling. The tenth day died William Bruster, Gentleman, of a wound given by the savages, and was buried the eleventh day.

The fourteenth day, Jerome Alikock, Ancient, died of a wound, the same day Francis Midwinter, Edward Moris, Corporal, died suddenly.

The fifteenth day, there died Edward Browne and Stephen Galthrope. The sixteenth day, there died Thomas Gower, Gentleman. The seventeenth day, there died Thomas Mounslic. The eighteenth day, there died Robert Pennington, and John Martine, Gentleman. The nineteenth day, died Drue Pigasse, Gentleman. The two and twentieth day of August, there died

Captain Bartholomew Gosnold, one of our Council; he was honorably buried, having all the ordinance in the fort shot off, with many volleys of small shot.

After Captain Gosnold's death, the Council could hardly agree by the dissension of Captain Kendall, which afterward was committed about heinous matters which was proved against him.

The four and twentieth day, died Edward Harington and George Walker, and were buried the same day. The six and twentieth day, died Kenelme Throgmortine. The seven and twentieth day died William Roods. The eight and twentieth day died Thomas Stoodie, Cape Merchant [supply officer].

The fourth day of September died Thomas Jacob, Sergeant. The fifth day, there died Benjamin Beast. Our men were destroyed with cruel diseases as swellings, fluxes, burning fevers, and by wars, and some departed suddenly, but for the most part they died of meer famine. There were never Englishmen left in a foreign country in such misery as we were in this new discovered Virginia. We watched every three nights, lying on the bare cold ground what weather soever came, warded all the next day, which brought our men to be most feeble wretches. Our food was but a small can of barley sod in water to five men a day; our drink cold water taken out of the river, which was at a flood very salty, at a low tide full of slime and filth, which was the destruction of many of our men. Thus, we lived for the space of five months in this miserable distress, not having five able men to man our bulwarks upon any occasion. If it had not pleased God to have put a terror in the savages' hearts, we had all perished by those wild and cruel pagans, being in that weak estate as we were, our men night and day groaning in every corner of the fort most pitiful to hear. If there were any conscience in men, it would make their hearts to bleed to hear the pitiful murmurings & outcries of our sick men, without relief, every night and day for the space of six weeks, some departing out of the World, many times three or four in a night, in the morning their bodies trailed out of their cabins like dogs to be buried. In this sort did I see the mortality of divers of our people.

It pleased God, after a while, to send those people which were our mortal enemies to relieve us with victuals, as bread, corn, fish, and flesh in great plenty, which was the setting up of our feeble men, otherwise we had all perished. Also we were frequented by divers kings in the country, bringing us store of provision to our great comfort.

The eleventh day, there was certain articles laid against Master Wingfield, which was then president. Thereupon he was not only displaced out of his presidentship, but also from being of the Council. Afterwards Captain John Ratcliffe was chosen president.

The eighteenth day, died one Ellis Kinistone, which was starved to death with cold. The same day at night, died one Richard Simmons. The nineteenth day, there died one Thomas Mouton. . . .

NOTES

1. Purchas, Samuel, *Haklutus Posthumus, or Purchas his Pilgrimes* (London: Imprinted for Henry Fetherston at the sign of the rose in Paul's church yard, 1625), 1685-90.
2. Miller, Lee, *Roanoke: Solving the Mystery of the Lost Colony* (New York: Arcade Publishing, 2001), 212-13. Miller uses this briefly mentioned episode as evidence for her theory that the survivors of the Lost Colony were scattered by war and the slave

trade throughout the tribes in North Carolina and Virginia.

3. Rountree, Helen C., *The Powhatan Indians of Virginia* (Norman: University of Oklahoma Press, 1989), 117. Although called Powhatan's Town, or simply Powhatan, this place was not the emperor Powhatan's primary residence, though it was probably the place of his birth. The town was ruled by Powhatan's son, Parahunt.

Politics on the Edge of the World

From
A Discourse of Virginia[1]
by Edward Maria Wingfield

> *Edward Maria Wingfield could have become one of
> the immortal figures in Virginia and American history.
> He was one of the first four patentees in the Virginia
> Company of London, the only one to undertake the voyage
> to Virginia himself, and he served as Jamestown's first
> president. He proved to be such an unpopular and
> ineffective leader, however, that he was deposed from the
> presidency and confined to a ship before the end of the
> first summer.[2] His life was probably saved only by the
> arrival of Captain Christopher Newport with the First
> Supply in the winter of 1608. When Newport returned to
> England, Wingfield was with him, and he never saw
> Virginia again.*

Wingfield wrote A Discourse of Virginia *to the Council of the Virginia Company of London as an attempt to salvage his standing, after his abrupt return from Jamestown and the reports of Gabriel Archer and others, whose ships managed to reach England first. Lacking the lively details of exploration that highlight the narratives of Smith and Percy, Wingfield's* Discourse *is nonetheless a breathtaking record of overwhelming pettiness in the midst of the direst circumstances.*

Right Worshipful and more worthy:

My due respect to yourselves, my allegiance (if I may so term it) to the Virginian action, my good heed to my poor reputation, thrust a pen into my hands, so jealous am I to be missing to any to them. If it wandereth in extravagances, yet shall they not be idle to those physicians whose loves have undertaken the safety and advancement of Virginia.

It is no small comfort that I speak before such gravity, whose judgment no fore-runner can forestall with any opprobrious untruths, whose wisdoms can easily disrobe malice out of her painted garments from the ever-reverenced truth.

I did so faithfully betroth my best endeavors to this noble enterprise, as my carriage might endure no suspicion. I never turned my face from danger, or hid my hands from labor; so watchful a sentinel stood myself to myself. I know well, a troop of errors continually besiege men's actions, some of them seized on by malice, some by ignorance. I do not hoodwink my carriage in my self-love, but freely and humbly submit it to your grave censures.

I do freely and truly anatomize the government and governors, that your experience may apply medicines accordingly, and upon the truth of this journal do pledge my faith and life, and so do rest.

Yours to command in all service.

Here followeth what happened in Jamestown, in Virginia, after Captain Newport's departure for England.

Captain Newport, having always his eyes and ears open to the proceedings of the Colony, three or four days before his departure asked the President [Wingfield] how he thought himself settled in the government, whose answer was, that no disturbance could endanger him or the Colony, but it must be wrought either by Captain Gosnold or Mister Archer; for the one was strong with friends and followers, and could if he would, and the other was troubled with an ambitious spirit, and would if he could.

The Captain gave them both knowledge of this, the President's opinion, and moved them, with many entreaties, to be mindful of their duties to His Majesty and the Colony.

June, 1607—The 22nd, Captain Newport returned for England, for whose good passage and safe return we made many prayers to our Almighty God.

June the 25th, an Indian came to us from the great Powhatan with the word of peace: that he desired greatly our friendship; that the werowances, Paspahegh and Tappahanna, should be our friends; that we should sow and reap in peace, or else he would make wars upon them with us. This message fell out true, for both those werowances have ever since remained in peace and trade with us. We rewarded the messenger with many trifles which were great wonders to him.

This Powhatan dwelleth 10 miles from us, upon the River Pamunkey, which lyeth north from us. The Powhatan in the former journal [Percy's] mentioned (a dweller by Captain Newport's falls) is a werowance, and under this Great Powhatan, which before we knew not.

July—The 3rd of July, seven or eight Indians presented the President a deer from Pamunkey, a werowance, desiring our friendship.[3] They enquired after our shipping [ships], which the President said was gone to Croatoan [North Carolina's Outer Banks]. They fear much our ships, and therefore he would not have them think it far from us. . . . A little after this came a deer to the President from the Great Powhatan. He and his messengers were pleased with the like trifles. The President likewise bought divers times deer of the Indians; beavers, and other flesh; which he always caused to be equally divided among the colony.

About this time, divers of our men fell sick. We missed above forty before September did see us, amongst whom was the worthy and religious gentleman Captain Bartholomew Gosnold, upon whose liefs [willingness] stood a great part of the good success and fortune of our government and colony. In his sickness time, the President did easily foretell his own deposing from his command, so much differed the President and the other councilors in managing the government of the colony. . . .

The . . . of . . . Mister Kendall was put off from being of the council, and committed to prison; for that it did manifestly appear he did practice to sow discord between the President and council.

Sickness had not now left us *vj* men in our town.[4] God's only mercy did now watch and ward for us. But the President hid this our weakness carefully from the savages, never suffering them, in all his time, to come into our town.

September—The *vj*th of September, Paspahegh sent us a boy that was run from us. This was the first assurance of his peace with us; besides, we found them no cannibals.

The boy observed the men and women to spend the most part of the night in singing or howling, and that every morning the women carried all the little children to the river's sides; but what they did there, he did not know.

The rest of the werowances do likewise send our men runnagats [renegades] to us home again, using them well during their being with them. So as now, they being well rewarded at home at their return, they take little joy to travel abroad without passports.

The council demanded some larger allowance for themselves, and for some sick, their favorites, which the President would not yield unto, without their warrants.

This matter was before propounded by Captain Martin, but so nakedly as that he neither knew the quantity of the store to be but for *xiij* weeks and a half, under the Cape Merchant's hand. He prayed them further to consider the long time before we expected Captain Newport's return; the uncertainty of his return, if God did not favor his voyage; the long time before our harvest would be ripe; and the doubtful peace that we had with the Indians, which they would keep no longer than opportunity served to do us mischief.

It was then therefore ordered that every meal of fish or flesh should excuse the allowance for porridge, both against the sick and whole. The council, therefore, sitting again upon this proposition, instructed in the former reasons and order, did not think fit to break the former order by enlarging their allowance, as will appear by the most voices ready to be showed under their hands. Now was the common store of oil, vinegar, sack [a strong wine], and aquavite [liquor] all spent, saving two gallons of each: the sack reserved for the Communion Table, the rest for such extremities as might fall upon us, which the President had only made known to Captain Gosnold, of which course he liked well. The vessels were therefore bunged up [broken, unusable]. When Mister Gosnold was dead, the President did acquaint the rest of the council with the said remnant. But, Lord, how they then longed for to sup up that little remnant! For they had now emptied all their own bottles, and all other that they could smell out.

A little while after this, the council did again fall upon the President for some better allowance for themselves, and some few the sick, their privates [friends]. The President protested he would not be partial; but, if one had any thing of him, every man should have his portion according to their place. Nevertheless, that, upon their warrants, he would deliver what pleased them to demand. If the President had at that time enlarged the portion according to their request, without doubt, in very short time, he had starved the whole company. He would not join with them, therefore, in such ignorant murder without their own warrant.

The President, well seeing to what end their impatience would grow, desired them earnestly and often times to bestow the Presidentship among themselves, that he would obey, a private man, as well as they could command. But they refused to discharge him of the place, saying they might not do it, for that he did his Majesty good service in it. In this meantime, the Indians did daily relieve us with corn and flesh, that, in three weeks, the President had reared up 20 men able to work; for, as his store increased, he mended the common pot. He had laid up, besides, provision for three weeks' wheat beforehand.

By this time, the council had fully plotted to depose

Wingfield, their then President, and had drawn certain articles in writing amongst themselves, and took their oaths upon the Evangelists to observe them. The effect whereof was, first—

To depose the then President;

To make Mister Ratcliffe the next President;

Not to depose the one the other;

Not to take the deposed President into council again;

Not to take Mister Archer into the council, or any other, without the consent of every one of them. To this they had subscribed, as out of their own mouths, at several times, it was easily gathered. Thus had they forsaken his Majesty's government, set us down in the instructions, and made it a Triumvirate [Ratcliffe, Martin, Smith].

It seemeth Mister Archer was nothing acquainted with these articles. Though all the rest crept out of his notes and commentaries that were preferred against the President, yet it pleased God to cast him into the same disgrace and pit that he prepared for another, as will appear hereafter.

September—the 10th of September, Mister Ratcliffe, Mister Smith, and Mister Martin came to the President's tent with a warrant, subscribed under their hands, to depose the President, saying they thought him very unworthy to be either President or of the council, and therefore discharged him of both. He answered them, that they had eased him of a great deal of care and trouble; that, long since, he had divers times proffered them the place at an easier rate; and, further, that the President ought to be removed (as appeareth in his Majesty's instructions for our government) by the greater number of *xiij* voices, councilors; that they were but three, and therefore wished them to proceed advisedly. But they told him, if they did him wrong, they must answer it. Then said the deposed President, "I am at your pleasure: dispose of me as you will, without further garboiles [confusions]."

I will now write what followeth in my own name, and give the new president his title. I shall be the briefer being thus discharged. I was committed to a sergeant, and sent to the pinnace . . .

The 11th of September, I was sent for to come before the President and council upon their court day. They had now made Mister Archer Recorder of Virginia. The President made a speech to the colony, that he thought it fit to acquaint them why I was deposed. I am now forced to stuff my paper with frivolous trifles, that our grave and worthy council [in London] may the better strike those veins where the corrupt blood lyeth, and that they may see in what manner of government the hope of the colony now travaileth.

First, Master President said that I had denied him a penny whittle [knife], a chicken, a spoonful of beer, and served him with foul corn; and with that pulled some grain out of a bag, showing it to the company.

Then start up Mister Smith, and said that I had told him plainly how he lied; and that I said, though we were equal here, yet, if he were in England, he would think scorn his man should be my companion.

Mister Martin followed with, "He reporteth that I do slack the service in the Colony, and do nothing but tend my pot, spit, and oven; but he hath starved my son, and denied him a spoonful of beer. I have friends in England shall be revenged on him, if ever he come in London."

I asked Mister President if I should answer these complaints, and whether he had ought else to charge me withall. With that he pulled out a paper book, loaded full with articles against me, and gave them [to] Mister Archer to read.

I told Mister President and the council that, by the instructions for our government, our proceedings ought to be verbal, and I was there ready to answer; but they said they would proceed in that order. I desired a copy of the articles, and time given me to answer them likewise by writing, but that would not be granted. I bade them then please themselves. Mister Archer then read some of the articles; when, on the sudden, Mister President said, "Stay, stay! We know not whether he will abide our judgment, or whether he will appeal to the King," saying to me, "How say you: Will you appeal to the King, or no?" I apprehended presently that God's mercy had opened me a way, through their ignorance, to escape their malice, for I never knew how I might demand an appeal. Besides, I had secret knowledge how they had forejudged me to pay five fold for any thing that came to my hands, whereof I could not discharge myself by writing, and that I should lie in prison until I had paid it.

The Cape Merchant had delivered me our merchandise, without any note of the particularities, under my hand, for himself had received them in gross. I likewise, as occasion moved me, spent them in trade or by gift amongst the Indians. So likewise did Captain Newport take of them, when he went up to discover the King's River, what he thought good, without any note of his hand mentioning the certainty, and disposed of them as was fit for him. Of these, likewise, I could make no account; only I was well assured I had never bestowed the value of three penny whittles to my own use, nor to the private use of any other, for I never carried any favorite over with me, or entertained any there. I was all one and one to all.

Upon these considerations, I answered Mister President and the council, that his Majesty's hands were full of mercy, and that I did appeal to his Majesty's mercy. They then committed me prisoner again to the master of ye pinnace, with these words, "Look to him well: he is now the King's prisoner."

Then Mister Archer pulled out of his bosom another paper book full of articles against me, desiring that he might read them in the name of the colony. I said I stood there ready to answer any man's complaint whom I had wronged; but no one man spoke one word against me. Then was he willed to read his book, whereof I complained; but I was still answered, "If they do me wrong, they must answer it." I have forgotten the most of the articles, they were so slight (yet he glorieth much in his penwork). I know well the last: and a speech that he then made savored well of a mutiny, for he desired that by no means I might lie prisoner in the town, lest both he and others of the colony should not give such obedience to their command as they ought to do: which goodly speech of his they easily swallowed.

But it was usual and natural to this honest gentleman, Mister Archer, to be always hatching of some mutiny in my time. He might have appeared an author of three several mutinies.

And he (as Mister Percy sent me word) had bought some witnesses' hands against me to divers articles, with Indian cakes (which was no great matter to do after my deposal, and considering their hunger), persuasions, and threats. At another time, he feared not to say openly, and in the presence of one of the council, that, if they had not deposed me when they did, he had gotten twenty others to himself which should have deposed me. But this speech of his was likewise easily desisted. Mister Crofts feared not to say that, if others would join with him, he would pull me out of my seat, and out of my skin, too. Others would say (whose names I spare) that, unless I would amend their allowance, they would be their own carvers. For these mutinous speeches I rebuked them openly, and proceeded no further against them, considering then of men's lives in the King's service there. One of the council was very earnest with me to take a guard about me. I answered him, I would no guard but God's love and my own innocence. In all these disorders was Mister Archer a ringleader.

When Mister President and Mister Archer had made an end of their articles above mentioned, I was again sent prisoner to the pinnace, and Mister Kendall, taken from thence, had his liberty, but might not carry arms.

All this while, the savages brought to the town such corn and flesh as they could spare. Paspahegh, by Tappahanna's mediation, was taken into friendship with us. The councilors, Mister Smith especially, traded up and down the river with the Indians for corn, which relieved the colony well.

As I understand by a report, I am much charged with starving the colony. I did always give every man his allowance faithfully, both of corn, oil, aquavite, etc., as was by the council proportioned. Neither was it bettered after my time, until, towards the end of March, a biscuit was allowed to every working man for his breakfast, by means of the provision brought us by Captain Newport, as will appear hereafter. It is further said I did much banquet and riot. I never had but one squirrel roasted, whereof I gave part to Mister Ratcliffe, then sick; yet was that squirrel given me. I did never heat a fleshpot but when the common pot was so used likewise. Yet how often Mister President's and the councilors' spits have night and day been endangered to break their backs, so laden with swans, geese, ducks, etc! How many times their fleshpots have swelled, many hungry eyes did behold, to their great longing? And what great thieves and thieving there hath been in the common store since my time, I doubt not but is already made known to his Majesty's Council for Virginia.

The 17th day of September, I was sent for to the court to answer a complaint exhibited against me by Jehu Robinson; for that, when I was president, I did say, he with others had consented to run away with the shallop to Newfoundland. At another time, I must answer Mister Smith for that I had said he did conceal an intended mutiny. I told Mister Recorder those words would bear no actions, that one of the causes was done without the limits mentioned in the patent granted to us, and therefore prayed Mister President that I might not be thus lugged with these disgraces and troubles. But he did wear no other eyes or ears than grew on Mister Archer's head.

The jury gave the one of them 100 pounds and the other 200 pound damages for slander. Then Mister Recorder did very learnedly comfort me, that, if I had wrong, I might bring my writ of error in London; whereat I smiled.

I, seeing their law so speedy and cheap, desired justice for a copper kettle which Mister Crofts did detain from me. He said I had given it him. I did bid him bring his proof for that. He confessed he had no proof. Then Mister President did ask me if I would be sworn I did not give it him. I said I knew no cause why to swear for mine own. He asked Mister Crofts if he would make oath I did give it him; which oath he took, and won my kettle from me, that was in that place and time worth half his weight in gold. Yet I did understand afterwards that he would have given John Capper the one half of the kettle to have taken the oath for him, but he would no copper on that price.

I told Mister President I had not known the like law, and prayed they would be more sparing of law until we had more wit or wealth; that laws were good spies in a populous, peaceable, and plentiful country, where they did make the good men better, and stayed the bad from being worse; yet we were so poor as they did but rob us of time that might be better employed in service in the Colony.

The . . . day of . . . the President did beat James Read, the smith. The smith struck him again. For this he was condemned to be hanged; but, before he was turned of the lather, he desired to speak with the President in private, to whom he accused Mister Kendall of a mutiny, and so escaped himself. What indictment Mister Recorder framed against the smith, I know not; but I know it is familiar for the President, councilors, and other officers to beat men at their pleasures. One lyeth sick till death, another walketh lame, the third cryeth out of all his bones, which miseries they do take upon their consciences to come to them by this their alms of beating. Were this whipping, lawing, beating, and hanging, in Virginia, known in England, I fear it would drive many well-affected minds from this honorable action of Virginia.

. . . The . . . day of . . ., Mister Kendall was executed, being shot to death for a mutiny. In the arrest of his judgment, he alleged to Mister President that his name was Sicklemore, not Ratcliffe, and so had no authority to pronounce judgment.[5] Then Mister Martin pronounced judgment.

Somewhat before this time, the President and council had sent for the keys of my coffers, supposing that I had some writings concerning the colony. I requested that the clerk of the council might see what they took out of my coffers, but they would not suffer him or any other. Under color hereof, they took my books of account, and all my notes that concerned the expenses of the colony, and instructions under the Cape Merchant's hand of the store of provision, divers other books & trifles of my own proper goods, which I could never recover. Thus was I made good prize on all sides.

The . . . day of . . ., the President commanded me to come on shore; which I refused, as not rightfully deposed, and desired that I might speak to him and the council in the presence of ten of the best sort of the gentlemen. With much entreaty, some of them were sent for. Then I told them I was determined to go into England to acquaint our council there with our weakness. I said further, their laws and government was such as I had no joy to live under them any longer; that I did much mislike their triumvirate having forsaken his Majesty's instructions for our government, and therefore prayed there might be more made of the council. I said further, I desired not to go into England, if either Mister President or Mister Archer would go, but was willing to take my fortune with the colony; and did also proffer to furnish them with 100 pounds towards the fetching home the colony, if the action was given over. They did like of none of my proffers, but made divers shout at me in the pinnace. I, seeing their resolutions, went ashore to them, where, after I had stayed awhile in conference, they sent me to the pinnace again.

The 10th of December, Mister Smith went up the river of the Chickahominies to trade for corn. He was desirous to see the head of that river; and, when it was not passable with the shallop, he hired a canoe and an Indian to carry him up further. The river the higher grew worse and worse. Then he went on shore with his guide, and left Robinson and Emry, two of our men, in the canoe; which were presently slain by the Indians, Pamunkey's men, and he himself taken prisoner, and, by the means of his guide, his life was saved; and Pamunkey, having him prisoner, carried him to his neighbors' werowances to see if any of them knew him for one of those which had been, some two or three years before us, in a river amongst them northward, and taken away some Indians from them by force. At last he brought him to the great Powhatan (of whom before we had no knowledge), who sent him home to our town the *viij* of January.

During Mister Smith's absence, the President did swear Mister Archer one of the council, contrary to his oath taken in the articles agreed upon between themselves (before spoken of), and contrary to the King's instructions, and without Mister Martin's consent; whereas there were no more but the President and Mister Martin then of the council.

Mister Archer, being settled in his authority, sought how to call Mister Smith's life in question, and had indicted him upon a chapter in Leviticus for the death of his two men. He had had his trial the same day of his return, and, I believe, his hanging the same or the next day, so speedy is our law there. But it pleased God to send Captain Newport unto us the same evening, to our unspeakable comfort, whose arrival saved Mister Smith's life and mine, because he took me out of the pinnace, and gave me leave to lie in the town. Also by his coming was prevented a parliament, which ye new councilor, Mister Recorder, intended there to summon. Thus error begot error.

Captain Newport, having landed, lodged, and refreshed his men, employed some of them about a fair storehouse, others about a stove [a drying room or kiln], and his mariners about a church; all which works they finished cheerfully and in short time.

The 7th of January, our town was almost quite burnt, with all our apparel and provision; but Captain Newport healed our wants, to our great comforts, out of the great plenty sent us by the provident and loving care of our worthy and most worthy council. . . .

By this time, the council & Captain, having intentively looked into the carriage both of the councilors and other officers, removed some officers out of the store, and Captain Archer, a councilor whose insolency did look upon that little himself with great sighted spectacles, derogating from others' merits by spewing out his venomous libels and infamous chronicles upon them, and other worse tricks, he had not escaped ye halter, but that Captain Newport interposed his advice to the contrary.

Captain Newport, having now dispatched all his business and set the clock in a true course (if so the council will keep it), prepared himself for England upon the 10th of April, and arrived at Blackwall on Sunday, the *xxj*th of May, 1608.

FINIS.

Notes

1. Wingfield, Edward-Maria, *A Discourse of Virginia, edited with notes and an introduction by Charles Deane* (Boston: J. Wilson and Son, 1860), 1-45.

2. Hume, Ivor Noel, *The Virginia Adventure: Roanoke to James Towne, An Archaeological and Historical Odyssey* (Charlottesville: University Press of Virginia, 1994), 128.

3. Rountree, Helen C., *The Powhatan Indians of Virginia* (Norman: University of Oklahoma Press, 1989), 117. Wingfield tends to refer to Native American leaders by the name of the tribe or place they rule, rather than by a personal name. Pamunkey was ruled by three of Powhatan's brothers, Opitchapam, Katatough, and Opechancanough; based on later accounts, Opechancanough was the most active of those three.

4. The editor was unsuccessful in his efforts to ascertain the significance of the italicized letters used throughout this text.

5. Hume, *The Virginia Adventure*, 164. "No historian has yet solved this mystery, though it has been suggested that Ratcliffe may have been another of the earl of Salisbury's secret agents, thus explaining the appointment of so shadowy a figure to the council."

Captian Smith Saves the Day

From

A True Relation of Such Occurrences and Accidents of Note as Hath Happened in Virginia Since the First Planting of that Colony, which is now resident in the South part thereof, till the last return from thence.

Written by Captain Smith, one of the said colony, to a worshipful friend of his in England[1]

The only episode in the Jamestown story that has entered the popular consciousness is that of John Smith and Pocahontas. Nobody has written a song about George Percy, and try finding a one-armed Christopher Newport doll at the Disney Store. Smith's A True Relation, *his first published account of his exploits in Virginia is most significant, then, for what it lacks: any mention at all of Pocahontas saving his life.*

Smith's A True Relation *is easily the most elaborate and exciting record of Jamestown's first year, in large part because Smith was the colony's most active member. Born a yeoman's son in the village of Willoughby, Smith had a catch-as-catch-can education and a brief apprenticeship before signing on to fight the Spanish in the Netherlands. Later, according to his favorite biographer (himself), Smith was fighting with the Austrians in their war against the Turks when he was captured and sold as a slave. Stripped, chained, and forced to work in the grain fields, his opportunity to escape came when his master came to beat him with a threshing bat. Smith took the weapon from the Turk, killed him with it, and somehow managed to make his way back to England in time to make himself a well-heard advocate for New World exploration. That advocacy, and his reputation as a soldier, convinced the Virginia Company to name him one of the first six councilors.*[2]

Having been charged with mutiny during the voyage over, Smith remained under restraint for almost a month after landing; only the diplomacy of the colony's minister, Robert Hunt, got him released. Once free, Smith quickly took over the exploration of Virginia, making almost constant trips to search out new routes, discover new rivers, and trade with the Indians for corn. As a result, Smith's account does not say much about events within the confines of Jamestown, but had Smith not been on the go, there would have been few events other than slow starvation to relate.

Pocahontas appears in A True Relation *only as the ten-year-old apple of her fearsome father's eye, and barely figures in the story of Smith's captivity. The dominant characters in* A True Relation, *apart from Smith, are*

Pocahontas's father Powhatan and her uncle Opechancanough. The English had been in Virginia for some time before they learned of Powhatan's existence, and his power, and no Englishman had met Powhatan (and lived to tell about it) until Smith was captured and taken before him. Powhatan was ruler of the vast Powhatan Empire, a collection of Algonquian tribes whose approximate borders were the fall line in eastern Virginia, the Potomac River in the north, and the Great Dismal Swamp to the south. The empire included most, but not all, of the region's tribes, who paid tribute to Powhatan.[3] Though Powhatan would prove himself a formidable adversary, his brother Opechancanough would eventually become the greater threat to Jamestown's survival. He is the "King of Pamunkey" who captures Smith and kills his two companions. Although he would later give away his niece in marriage to an Englishman, he remained a more implacable enemy to the English than his brother. Opechancanough launched surprise attacks in 1622 and 1644 that nearly succeeded in wiping out the colony. He was captured after the 1644 attack. The Virginians planned to send him to England, so that he could be paraded before the King and locked in the Tower of London. While under guard in Jamestown, though, Opechancanough—more than 90 years old, unable to walk, and blind—was shot in the back and killed.

Kind Sir, commendations remembered, etc.
You shall understand that after many crosses in the downs

by tempests, we arrived safely upon the southwest part of the great Canaries. Within four or five days after, we set sail for Dominica, the 26th Of April. The first land we made, we fell with Cape Henry, the very mouth of the Bay of Chesapeake, which at that present we little expected, having by a cruel storm been put to the northward.

Anchoring in this bay, twenty or thirty went ashore with the Captain, and in coming aboard [ashore], they were assaulted with certain Indians, which charged them within pistol shot; in which conflict, Captain Archer and Matthew Morton were shot. Whereupon, Captain Newport, seconding them, made a shot at them, which the Indians little respected, but having spent their arrows retired without harm. And in that place was the box opened, wherin the Council for Virginia was nominated. And arriving at the place where we are now seated, the council was sworn; the president elected, which for that year was Master Edward Maria Wingfield; where was made choice for our situation a very fit place for the erecting of a great city, about which some contention passed betwixt Captain Wingfield and Captain Gosnold. Notwithstanding, all our provision was brought ashore, and with as much speed as might be, we went about our fortification.

The two and twenty day of April, Captain Newport and myself, with divers others to the . . . number of twenty-two persons, set forward to discover the [James] river, some fifty or sixty miles, finding it in some places broader, and in some narrower; the country (for the most part) on each side plain high ground, with many fresh springs, the people in all places kindly treating us, dancing and feasting us with strawberries, mulberries, bread, fish, and other [of] their country provisions whereof we had plenty, for which Captain Newport kindly requited their least favors with bells, pins, needles, beads, or glasses, which so contented them that his liberalities made them follow us from place to place, ever kindly to respect us. In the midway, staying to refresh ourselves in little isle, four or five savages came unto us, which described unto us the course of the river, and after in our journey they often met us, trading with us for such provision as we had. And arriving at Arsateck, he whom we supposed to be the chief king of all the rest most kindly entertained us, giving us in a guide to go with us up the river to Powhatan, of which place their great emperor taketh his name, where he that they honored for king used us kindly. But to finish this discovery, we passed on further, where within a mile we were intercepted with great craggy stones in the midst of the river, where the water falleth so rudely, and with such a violence, as not any boat can possibly pass; and so broad disperseth the stream, as there is not past five or six foot at a low water, and to the shore scarce passage with a barge. The water floweth four foot, and the freshes by reason of the rocks have left marks of the inundation eight or nine foot. The south side high mountains, the rocks being of gravelly nature, interlaced with many veins of glisterling spangles.

That night we returned to Powhatan. The next day (being Whitsunday after dinner) we returned to the falls, leaving a mariner in pawn with the Indians for a guide of theirs. He that they honored for king followed us by the river (further he would not go), so there we erected a cross, and that night, taking our man at Powhatan's, Captain Newport congratulated his kindness with a gown and a hatchet. Returning to Arsateck, and stayed there the next day to observe the height thereof, and so, with many signs of love, we departed. . . .

That night, passing by Weyanoke some twenty miles from

our fort, they, according to their former churlish condition, seemed little to affect us, but as we departed and lodged at the point of Weyanoke, the people the next morning seemed kindly to content us, yet we might perceive many signs of a more jealousy in them than before, and also the hind that the King of Arsateck had given us, altered his resolution in going to our fort, and with many kind circumstances left us there. This gave us some occasion to doubt some mischief at the fort, yet Captain Newport intended to have visited Paspahegh and Tappahannock, but the instant change of the wind being fair for our return we repaired to the fort with all speed, where the first we heard was that 400 Indians the day before assaulted the fort, and surprised it. Had not God (beyond all their expectations) by means of the ships, at whom they shot with their ordinances and muskets, caused them to retire, they had entered the fort with our own men, which were then busied in setting corn, their arms being then in dry fats [large containers] and few ready but certain gentlemen of their own. In which conflict, most of the council was hurt, a boy slain in the pinnace, and thirteen or fourteen more hurt. With all speed we pallisadoed our fort. For six or seven days we had alarums by ambuscadoes, and four or five cruelly wounded by being abroad. The Indians' loss we know not, but as they report three were slain and divers hurt.

Captain Newport, having set things in order, set sail for England the 22nd of June, leaving provision for 13 or 14 weeks. The day before the ships' departure, the king of Pamunkey sent the Indian that had met us before in our discovery to assure us peace, our fort being then pallisadoed round, and all our men in good health and comfort; albeit, that through some discontented humors, it did not so long continue. For the president and Captain Gosnold, with the rest of the council, being for the most part discontented with one another, in so much that things were neither carried with that discretion, nor any business effected in such good sort, as wisdom would, nor our own good and safety required thereby, and through the hard dealings of our president, the rest of the council being diversely affected through his audacious command, and for Captain Martin, albeit very honest and wishing the best good, yet so sick and weak, and myself disgraced through others' malice, through which disorder God (being angry with us) plagued us with such famine and sickness that the living were scarce able to bury the dead. Our want of sufficient and good victuals, with continual watching four or five each night at three bulwarks, being the chief cause. Only of sturgeon we had great store, whereon our men would so greedily surfeit, as it cost many their lives. The sack, aquavite, and other preservatives for our health, being kept only in the president's hands, for his own diet, and his few associates.

Shortly after, Captain Gosnold fell sick, and within three weeks died. Captain Ratcliffe being then also very sick and weak, and myself having also tasted of the extremity therof, but by God's assistance being well recovered. Kendall, about this time, for divers reasons deposed from being of the council. And shortly after it pleased God (in our extremity) to move the Indians to bring us corn, ere it was half ripe, to refresh us, when we rather expected when they would destroy us.

About the tenth of September there was about 46 of our men dead, at which time Captain Wingfield, having ordered the affairs in such sort that he was generally hated of all, in which respect with one consent he was deposed from his presidency, and Captain Ratcliffe according to his course was elected.

Our provision now being within twenty days spent, the Indians brought us great store both of corn and bread ready made. And also there came such abundance of fowls into the rivers, as greatly refreshed our weak estates, whereupon many of our weak men were presently able to go abroad.

As yet we had no houses to cover us. Our tents were rotten and our cabins worse than nought. Our best commodities was iron, which we made into little chisels.

The president, and Captain Martin's sickness, [required] me to be Cape Merchant, and yet to spare no pains in making houses for the company, who, notwithstanding our misery, little ceased their malice, grudging and muttering.

As at this time were most of our chiefest men either sick or discontented, the rest being in such despair as they would rather starve and rot with idleness than be persuaded to do anything for their own relief, without constraint. Our victuals being now within eighteen days spent, and the Indians' trade decreasing, I was sent to the mouth of the river to Kecoughtan, an Indian town, to trade for corn, and try the river for fish. But our fishing we could not effect, by reason of the stormy weather. The Indians, thinking us near famished, with careless kindness, offered us little pieces of bread and small handfuls of beans or wheat, for a hatchet or a piece of copper. In like manner I entertained their kindness, and in like scorn offered them like commodities; but the children, or any that showed extraordinary kindness, I liberally confronted with free gift such trifles as well contented them.

Finding this cold comfort, I anchored before the town, and the next day returned to trade, but God (the absolute disposer of all hearts) altered their conceits, for now they were no less desirous of our commodities than we of their corn . . . With fish, oysters, bread, and deer, they kindly traded with me and my men, being no less in doubt of my intent, than I of theirs; for well I might with twenty men have freighted a ship with corn. The town containeth eighteen houses pleasantly seated upon three acres of ground, upon a plain, half environed with a great bay of the great river, the other part with a bay of the other river falling into the great bay, with a little isle fit for a castle in the mouth thereof, the town adjoining to the main by a neck of land of sixty yards.

With sixteen bushels of corn I returned towards our fort. By the way I encountered with two canoes of Indians, who came aboard me, being the inhabitants of Warraskoyack, a kingdom on the south side of the river, which is in breadth five miles and 20 mile or near from the mouth. With these I traded, who having but their hunting provision, requested me to return to their town, where I should load my boat with corn. And with near thirty bushels I returned to the fort, the very name wherof gave great comfort to our despairing company.

Time thus passing away, and having not above 14 days victuals left, some motions were made about our President's and Captain Archer's going for England, to procure a supply; in which meantime we had reasonably fitted us with houses. And our President and Captain Martin being able to walk abroad, with much ado it was concluded that the pinnace and barge should go towards Powhatan, to trade for corn.

Lots were cast who should go in her. The chance was mine; and while she was a-rigging, I made a voyage to Tappahannock, where arriving, there was but certain women and children who fled from their houses, yet at last I drew them to draw near. Truck they durst not, corn they had plenty, and to spoil I had no commission.

In my return through Paspahegh, I traded with that churlish and treacherous nation. Having loaded 10 or 12 bushels of corn, they offered to take our pieces and swords. Yet by stealth, but seeming to dislike it, they were ready to assault us. Yet standing upon our guard, in coasting the shore divers out of the woods would meet with us with corn and trade. But lest we should be constrained either to endure overmuch wrong or directly fall to revenge, seeing them dog us from place to place, it being night, and our necessity not fit for wars, we took occasion to return with 10 bushels of corn.

Captain Martin after made two journeys to that nation of Paspahegh, but each time returned with eight or 10 bushels.

All things being now ready for my journey to Powhatan, for the performance thereof I had eight men and myself for the barge, as well for discovery as trading; [in] the pinnace [were] five mariners and two landmen to take in our landings at convenient places.

The ninth of November I set forward for the discovery of the country of Chickahominy, leaving the pinnace the next tide to follow, and stay for my coming at Point Weyanoke 20 miles from our fort. The mouth of this river falleth into the great river at Paspahegh, eight miles above our fort.

That afternoon I stayed the ebb in the bay of Paspahegh with the Indians. Towards the evening certain Indians hailed me; one of them, being of Chickahominy, offered to conduct me to his country. The Paspaheghans grudged thereat. Along we went by moonlight. At midnight he brought us before his town, desiring one of our men to go up with him, whom he kindly entertained, and returned back to the barge.

The next morning I went up to the town and showed them what copper and hatchets they should have for corn, each family seeking to give me most content. So long they caused me to stay that 100 at least was expecting my homecoming by the river, with corn. What I liked, I bought; and lest they should perceive my too great want, I went higher up the river.

This place is called Manosquosick, a quarter of a mile from the river, containing thirty or forty houses upon an exceeding high land. At the foot of the hill, towards the river, is a plain wood, watered with many springs, which fall twenty yards right down into the river. Right against the same is a great marsh, of four or five miles circuit, divided in two islands by the parting of the river, abounding with fish and fowl of all sorts.

A mile from thence is a town called Oraniocke. I further discovered the towns of Mansa, Apanaock, Werawahone, and Mamanahunt, at each place kindly used, especially at the last, being the heart of the country, where were assembled 200 people with such abundance of corn as, having laded our barge, as also I might have laded a ship.

I returned to Paspahegh, and considering the want of corn at our fort, it being night, with the ebb, by midnight I arrived at our fort ... The next morning I unladed seven hogsheads [large casks] into our store.

The next morning I returned again. The second day I arrived at Mamanahunt, where the people, having heard of my coming, were ready with three or four hundred baskets little and great, of which having laded my barge, with many signs of great kindness I returned.

At my departure they requested me to hear our pieces, being in the midst of the river, which in regard of the echo seemed a peal of ordinance. Many birds and fowls they see us daily kill that much feared them. So desirous of trade were they that they would follow me with their canoes, and for any thing, give it me, rather then return it back. So I unladed again seven or eight hogsheads at our fort.

Having thus by God's assistance gotten good store of corn, notwithstanding, some bad spirits, not content with God's providence, still grew mutinous; in so much that our president, having occasion to chide the smith for his misdemeanor, he not only gave him bad language, but also offered to strike him with some of his tools. For which rebellious act, the smith was by a jury condemned to be hanged. But being upon the ladder, continuing very obstinate as hoping upon a rescue, when he saw no other way but death with him, he became penitent, and declared a dangerous conspiracy. For which, Captain Kendall, as principal, was by a jury condemned, and shot to death.

This conspiracy appeased, I set forward for the discovery of the river Chickahominy. This third time I discovered the towns of Matapamient, Morinogh, Asacap, Moysenock, Righkahauck, Nechanichock, Mattalunt, Attamuspincke, and divers others. Their plenty of corn I found decreased, yet lading the barge, I returned to our fort.

Our store being now indifferently well provided with corn, there was much ado for to have the pinnace go for England, against which Captain Martin and myself stood chiefly against it. And in *fine*, after many debatings *pro et contra*, it was resolved to stay a further resolution.

This matter also quieted, I set forward to finish this discovery, which as yet I had neglected in regard of the necessity we had to take in provision whilst it was to be had. Forty miles I passed up the river, which for the most part is a quarter of a mile broad, and three fathom and a half deep, exceedy oozy, many great low marshes, and many high lands, especially about the midst at a place called Moysenock, a peninsula of four miles circuit, betwixt two rivers joined to the main by the neck of 40 or 50 yards from the high water mark. On both sides, on the very neck of the main, are high hills and dales, yet much inhabited, the isle declining in a plain fertile cornfield, the lower end a low marsh. More plenty of swans, cranes, geese, ducks, and mallards, and divers sorts of fowls, none would desire. More plain fertile planted ground, in such great proportions as there, I had not seen: of a light black sandy mold, the cliffs commonly red, white, and yellow colored sand, and under, red and white clay; fish, great plenty, and people in abundance. The most of their inhabitants [live] in view of the neck of land, where a better seat for a town cannot be desired.

At the end of forty miles, this river environeth many low islands at each high water drowned, for a mile, where it uniteth itself at a place called Apokant, the highest town inhabited.

Ten miles higher I discovered with the barge. In the mid way, a great tree hindered my passage, which I cut in two. Here the river became narrower, eight, nine, or 10 foot at a high water, and six or seven at a low; the stream exceeding swift, and the bottom hard channel; the ground, most part a low plain, sandy soil. This occasioned me to suppose it might issue from some lake or some broad ford, for it could not be far to the head, but rather then I would endanger the barge. Yet to have been able to resolve this doubt, and to discharge the imputation of malicious tongues, that half suspected I durst not, for so long delaying, some of the company, as desirous as myself, we resolved to hire a canoe, and return with the barge to Apokant, there to leave the barge secure, and put ourselves upon the adventure: the country only a vast and wild wilderness, and but only that town.

Within three or four mile, we hired a canoe, and two Indians to row us the next day a-fowling. Having made such provision for the barge as was needful, I left her there to ride, with express charge not any to go ashore till my return.

Though some wise men may condemn this too-bold attempt of too much indiscretion, yet if they well consider the friendship of the Indians in conducting me, the desolateness of the country, the probability of some lack, and the malicious judges of my actions at home, as also to have some matters of worth to encourage our adventurers in England, might well have caused any honest mind to have done the like, as well for his own discharge as for the public good.

Having two Indians for my guide and two of our own company, I set forward, leaving seven in the barge.

Having discovered 20 miles further in the desert, the river still kept his depth and breadth, but much more combred with trees.

Here we went ashore (being some 12 miles higher than the barge had been) to refresh ourselves during the boiling of our vituals. One of the Indians I took with me to see the nature of the soil, and to cross the boughts of the river. The other Indian I left with Master Robinson and Thomas Emry, with their matches lit, and order to discharge a piece, for my retreat, at the first sight of any Indian.

But within a quarter of an hour I heard a loud cry, and a hollowing of Indians, but no warning piece. Supposing them surprised, and that the Indians had betrayed us, presently I seized him and bound his arm fast to my hand in a garter, with my pistol ready bent to be revenged on him. He advised me to fly, and seemed ignorant of what was done.

But as we went discoursing, I was struck with an arrow on the right thigh, but without harm. Upon this occasion I espied two Indians drawing their bows, which I prevented in discharging a French pistol.

By that I had charged again, three or four more did the like; for the first fell down and fled. At my discharge, they did the like. My hind [prisoner] I made my barricado, who offered not to strive. Twenty or 30 arrows were shot at me, but short. Three or four times I had discharged my pistol ere the king of Pamunkey, called Opechancanough, with 200 men environed me, each drawing their bow. Which done, they laid them upon the ground, yet without shot.

My hind treated betwixt them and me of conditions of peace; he discovered me to be the captain. My request was to retire to the boat; they demanded my arms. The rest, they said, were slain; only me they would reserve.

The Indian importuned me not to shoot. In retiring, being in the midst of a low quagmire, and minding them more than my steps, I stepped fast into the quagmire . . .

Thus surprised, I resolved to try their mercies. My arms I cast from me, till which none durst approach me.

Being seized on me, they drew me out and led me to the king. I presented him with a compass dial, describing by my best means the use thereof. Whereat he so amazedly admired, as he suffered me to proceed in a discourse of the roundness of the earth, the course of the sun, moon, stars and planets.

With kind speeches and bread he requited me, conducting me where the canoe lay and John Robinson slain, with 20 or 30 arrows in him. Emry I saw not.

I perceived by the abundance of fires all over the woods. At each place I expected when they would execute me, yet they used me with what kindness they could.

Approaching their town, which was within six miles [of] where I was taken, only made as arbors and covered with mats, which they remove as occasion requires. All the women and children, being advertised of this accident, came forth to meet them, the king well guarded with 20 bowmen, five flank and rear, and each flank before him a sword and a piece, and after him the like, then a bowman, then I, on each hand a bowman, the rest in file in the rear, which rear led forth amongst the trees . . . each his bow and a handful of arrows, a quiver at his back grimly painted. On each flank a sergeant, the one running always towards the front, the other towards the rear, each a true pace and in exceeding good order.

This being a good time continued, they cast themselves in a ring with a dance, and so each man departed to his lodging.

The captain conducting me to his lodging, a quarter of venison and some ten pound of bread I had for supper. What I left was reserved for me, and sent with me to my lodging . . . My gown, points, and garters, my compass and my tablet they gave me again. Though eight ordinarily guarded me, I wanted not what they could devise to content me, and still our longer acquaintance increased our better affection.

Much they threatened to assault our fort, as they were solicited by the King of Paspahegh, who showed at our fort great signs of sorrow for this mischance. The king took great delight in understanding the manner of our ships, sailing the seas, the earth and skies, and of our God. What he knew of the dominions he spared not to acquaint me with, as of certain men . . . at a place called Ocanahonan, clothed like me; the course of our river, and that within four or five days' journey of the falls was a great turning of salt water.[4]

I desired he would send a messenger to Paspahegh (the district in which Jamestowne was situated), with a letter I would write, by which they should understand how kindly they used me, and that I was well, lest they should revenge my death. This he granted and sent three men, in such weather as in reason were unpossible by any naked to be endured . . .

The next day after my letter, came a savage to my lodging with his sword, to have slain me. But being by my guard intercepted, with a bow and arrow he offered to have effected his purpose. The cause I knew not, till the king, understanding thereof, came and told me of a man a-dying, wounded with my pistol. He told me also of another I had slain . . . This was the father of him I had slain, whose fury to prevent, the king presently conducted me to another kingdom, upon the top of the next northerly river called Yaughtawnoone . . .

Arriving at Werawocomoco, their emperor proudly lying upon a bedstead a foot high, upon ten or twelves mats, richly hung with many chains of great pearls about his neck, and covered with a great covering . . . At head sat a woman, at his feet another; on each side, sitting upon a mat upon the ground, were ranged his chief men on each side of the fire, ten in a rank, and behind them as many young women, each a great chain of white beads over their shoulders, their heads painted in red. And with such a grave and majestical countenance, as drove me into admiration to see such state in a naked savage.

He kindly welcomed me with such good words, and great platters of sundry victuals, assuring me his friendship, and my liberty within four days. He much delighted in Opechancanough's relation of what I had described to him, and oft examined me upon the same. (For more information, see "Pocahontas Saves Captain Smith.")

He asked me the cause of our coming.

I told him, being in fight with Spaniards our enemy, being overpowered, near put to retreat, and by extreme weather put to this shore. Where, landing at Chesapeake, the people shot us, but Kecoughtan they kindly used us. We by signs demanded fresh water, they described us up the river was all fresh water. At Paspahegh also they kindly used us; our pinnace being leaky, we were enforced to stay to mend her, till Captain Newport my father came to conduct us away.[5]

He demanded why we went further with our boat. I told him, in that I would have occasion to talk of the back sea, that on the other side the main, where was salt water: my father had a child slain, which we supposed Monocan his enemy, whose death we intended to revenge.

After good deliberation, he began to describe me the countries beyond the falls, with many of the rest; confirming what not only Opechancanough, and an Indian which had been prisoner to Powhatan had before told me. But some called it five days, some six, some eight, where the said water dashed amongst many stones and rocks, each storm, which caused oft times the head of the river to be brackish.

Anchanachuck he described to be the people that had slain my brother, whose death he would revenge. He described also, upon the same sea, a mighty nation called Pocoughtronack, a fierce nation that did eat men, and warred with the people of Moyaoncer and Pataromerke, nations upon the top of the head of the bay, under his territories, where the year before they had slain a hundred. He signified their crowns were shaven, long hair in the neck, tied on a knot, swords like poleaxes.

Beyond them, he described people with short coats, and sleeves to the elbows, that passed that way in ships like ours. Many kingdoms he described me, to the head of the bay, which seemed to be a mighty river issuing from mighty mountains betwixt the two seas. The people clothed at Ocanahonan, he also confirmed; and the southerly countries also, as the rest that reported us to be within a day and a half of Mangoge, two days of Chawanoac, six from Roanoke, to the south part of the back sea. He described a country called Anone, where they have abundance of brass, and houses walled as ours.[6]

I requited his discourse (seeing what pride he had in his great and spacious dominions, seeing that all he knew were under his territories) in describing to him the territories of Europe, which was subject to our great king whose subject I was, the innumerable multitude of his ships. I gave him to understand the noise of trumpets, and terrible manner of fighting were under Captain Newport my father, whom I entitled the Meworames, which they call the king of all the waters. At his greatness, he admired, and not a little feared. He desired me to forsake Paspahegh, and to live with him upon his river . . . He promised to give me corn, venison, or what I wanted to feed us. Hatchets and copper we should make him, and none should disturb us. This request I promised to perform; and thus, having with all the kindness he could devise sought to content me, he sent me home with four men: one that usually carried my gown and knapsack after me, two other loaded with bread, and one to accompany me. . . .

Powhatan hath three brethren, and two sisters, each of his brethren succeeded other. For the crown, their heirs inherit not, but the first heirs of the sisters, and so successively the women's heirs. For the kings have as many women as they will; his subjects two, and most but one.

From Werawocomoco (to Jamestown) is but 12 miles, yet the Indians trifled away that day, and would not go to our fort by any persuasions, but in certain old hunting houses of Paspahegh we lodged all night.

The next morning, ere sunrise, we set forward to our fort, where we arrived within an hour. . . . Each man, with the truest signs of joy they could express, welcomed me, except Master Archer, and some two or three of his, who was then in my absence sworn councilor, though not with the consent of Captain Martin.

Great blame and imputation was laid upon me by them, for the loss of our two men which the Indians slew, in so much that they purposed to depose me. But in the midst of my miseries, it pleased God to send Captain Newport, who, arriving there the same night, so tripled our joy as for a while these plots against me were deferred; though with much malice against me, which Captain Newport in short time did plainly see. Now was Master Scrivener, Captain Martin, and myself called councilors.

Within five or six days after the arrival of the ship, by a mischance our fort was burned, and the most of our apparel, lodging, and private provision. Many of our old men, diseased, and of our new want of lodging, perished.

The Emperor Powhatan, each week once or twice, sent me many presents of deer . . . half always for my father, whom he much desired to see, and half for me. And so continually importuned, by messengers and presents, that I would come to fetch the corn, and take the country their king had given me, as at last Captain Newport resolved to go see him.

Such acquaintance I had amongst the Indians, and such confidence they had in me, as near the fort they would not come till I came to them. Every of them, calling me by my name, would not sell anything till I had first received their presents, and what they had that I liked. They deferred to my discretion, but after acquaintance, they usually came into the fort at their pleasure. The president and the rest of the council, they knew not, but

Captain Newport's greatness I had so described, as they conceived him the chief, the rest his children, officers, and servants.

We had agreed with the king of Paspahegh to conduct two of our men to a place called Panawicke beyond Roanoke, where he reported many men to be apparelled. We landed him at Warraskoyack, where, playing the villain, and deluding us for rewards, returned within three or four days after, without going further.

Captain Newport, Master Scrivener, and myself, found the mouth of Pamunkey's river, some 25 or 30 miles northward from Cape Henry, the channel good as before expressed.

Arriving at Werawocomoco, being jealous of the intent of this politic savage, to discover his intent the better, I with 20 shot armed in jacks [leather armor] went ashore. The bay where he dwelleth hath in it three creeks, and a mile and a half from the channel, all ooze. Being conducted to the town, I found myself mistaken in the creek, for they all there were within less than a mile: the Emperor's son called Naukaquawis, the captain that took me, and divers others of his chief men, conducted me to their king's habitation. But in the mid way I was intercepted by a great creek over which they had made a bridge of grained stakes and rails. The king of Kiskiak, and Namontack, who all the journey the king had sent to guide us, had conducted us this passage, which caused me to suspect some mischief. The barge I had sent to meet me at the right landing, when I found myself first deceived. And knowing by experience the most of their courages to proceed from others' fear, though few liked the passage, I intermingled the king's son, our conductors, and his chief men amongst ours, and led forward, leaving half at the one end to make a guard for the passage of the front. The

Indians, seeing the weakness of the bridge, came with a canoe, and took me in of the middest, with four or five more. Being landed, we made a guard for the rest till all were passed.

Two in a rank we marched to the emperor's house. Before his house stood forty or fifty great platters of fine bread. Being entered the house, with loud tunes they all made signs of great joy. This proud savage, having his finest women, and the principal of his chief men assembled, sat in ranks as before is expressed, himself as upon a throne at the upper end of the house, with such a majesty as I cannot express, nor yet have often seen, either in pagan or Christian. With a kind countenance he bade me welcome, and caused a place to be made by himself (for me) to sit.

I presented him a suit of red cloth, a white greyhound, and a hat. As jewels he esteemed them, and with a great oration made by three of his nobles, if there be any amongst savages, kindly accepted them, with a public confirmation of a perpetual league and friendship.

After that he commanded the Queen of Appomattoc, a comely young savage, to give me water, a turkey cock, and bread to eat.

Being thus feasted, he began his discourse to this purpose, "Your kind visitation doth much content me, but where is your father whom I much desire to see, is he not with you?"

I told him he remained aboard, but the next day he would come unto him.

With a merry countenance he asked me for certain pieces which I promised him when I went to Paspahegh.

I told, according to my promise, that I proferred the man that went with me four demi-culverins, in that he so desired a great gun, but they refused to take them.

Whereat, with a loud laughter, he desired to give him some of less burden. As for the other, I gave him them, being sure that none could carry them. "But where are these men you promised to come with you?"

I told him, without. Who thereupon gave order to have them brought in, two after two, ever maintaining the guard without. And as they presented themselves, ever with thanks he would salute me, and caused each of them to have four or five pound of bread given them.

This done, I asked him for the corn and ground he promised me.

He told me I should have it; but he expected to have all these men lay their arms at his feet, as did his subjects.

I told him that was a ceremony our enemies desired, but never our friends, as we presented ourselves unto him; yet that he should not doubt of our friendship. The next day my father would give him a child of his, in full assurance of our loves, and not only that, but when he should think it convenient, we would deliver under his subjection in the country of Monacan and Pocoughtaonack his enemies.

This so contented him, as immediately, with attentive silence, with a loud oration he proclaimed me a Werowance of Powhatan, and that all his subjects should so esteem us, and no man account us strangers nor Paspahegans, but Powhatans, and that the corn, women, and country should be to us as to his own people. This proffered kindness, for many reasons, we condemned not, but with the best languages and signs of thanks I could express, I took my leave.

The King, rising from his seat, conducted me forth, and caused each of my men to have as much more bread as he could bear, giving me corn in a basket, and as much he sent a board for a present to my father. Victuals, you must know, is all their wealth, and the greatest kindness they could show us.

Arriving at the river, the barge was fallen so low with the ebb, though I had given order and oft sent to prevent the same; yet the messengers deceived me. The skies being very thick and rainy, the King, understanding this mischance, sent his son and Namontack to conduct me to a great house sufficient to lodge me; where entering, I saw it hung round with bows and arrows.

The Indians used all diligence to make us fires, and give us content. The king's orators presently entertained us with a kind oration, with express charge that not any should steal, or take our bows or arrows, or offer any injury.

Presently after he sent me a quarter of venison to stay my stomach.

In the evening, he sent for me to come only with two shot with me. The company I gave order to stand upon their guard, and to maintain two sentries at the ports all night.

To my supper he set before me meat for twenty men, and seeing I could not eat, he caused it to be given to my men; for this is a general custom, that what they give, not to take again, but you must either eat it, give it away, or carry it with you. Two or three hours we spent in our . . . discourses; which done, I was with a fire stick lighted to my lodging.

The next day the King conducted me to the river, showed me his canoes, and described unto me how he sent them over the bay for tribute beads, and also what countries paid him beads, copper, or skins.

But seeing Captain Newport and Master Scrivener coming ashore, the King returned to his house, and I went to meet them. With a trumpet before them, we marched to the King, who after his old manner kindly received them, especially a boy of thirteen years old, called Thomas Savage, whom he gave him as his son.[7] He requited this kindness with . . . a great basket of beans. And entertaining him with the former discourse, we passed away that day, and agreed to bargain the next day, and so returned to our pinnace.

The next day, coming ashore in like order, the King, having kindly entertained us with a breakfast, questioned us in this manner: why we came armed in that sort, seeing he was our friend, and had neither bows nor arrows; what did we doubt?

I told him it was the custom of our country, not doubting of his kindness any ways; wherewith, though he seemed satisfied, yet Captain Newport caused all our men to retire to the water side, which was some thirty score from thence.

But to prevent the worst, Master Scrivener or I were either the one or the other by the barge. Experience had well taught me to believe his friendship till convenient opportunity suffered him to betray us. But quickly this politician had perceived my absence, and cunningly sent for me; I sent for Master Scrivener to supply my place. The King would demand for him; I would again relieve him. And they sought to satisfy our suspicion with kind language, and not being agreed to trade for corn, he desired to see all our hatchets and copper together, for which he would give us corn. With that ancient trick the Chickahominians had oft acquainted me. His offer I refused, offering first to see what he would give for one piece. He, seeming to despise the nature of a merchant, did scorn to sell, but we freely should give him, and he liberally would requite us.

Captain Newport would not with less then twelve great coppers try his kindness, which he liberally requited with as much corn as at Chickahominy I had for one of less proportion. Our hatchets he would also have at his own rate, for which kindness he much seemed to affect Captain Newport. Some few bunches of blue beads I had, which he much desired, and seeing so few, he offered me a basket of two pecks, and that I drew to be three pecks at the least, and yet seemed contented and desired more. I agreed with him, the next day, for two bushels, for the ebb now constrained us to return to our boat, although he earnestly desired us to stay dinner which was a-providing; and being ready, he sent aboard after us, which was bread and venison sufficient for fifty or sixty persons.

The next day he sent his son in the morning, not to bring ashore with us any pieces, lest his women and children should fear. Captain Newport's good belief would have satisfied that request. Yet twenty or twenty-five shot we got ashore, the King importuning me to leave my arms aboard, much misliking my sword, pistol and target. I told him the men that slew my brother with the like terms had persuaded me, and being unarmed shot at us, and so betrayed us.

He oft entreated Captain Newport that his men might leave their arms, which still he commanded to the water side.

This day we spent in trading for blue beads, and having near freighted our barge, Captain Newport returned with them that came aboard, leaving me and Master Scrivener ashore, to follow in canoes. Into one I got with six of our men, which being launched, a stone's cast from the shore stuck fast in the ooze.

Master Scrivener, seeing this example, with seven or eight more passed the dreadful bridge, thinking to have found deeper water on the other creek. But they were enforced to stay, with such entertainment as a savage being forced ashore with wind and rain, having in his canoe, as commonly they have, his house and household, instantly set up a house of mats, which succoured them from the storm.

The Indians, seeing me pestered in the ooze, called to me. Six or seven of the King's chief men threw off their skins, and to the middle in ooze, came to bear me out on their heads. Their importunacy caused me better to like the canoe than their courtesy, excusing my denial for fear to fall into the ooze, desiring them to bring me some wood, fire, and mats to cover me, and I would content them. Each presently gave his help to satisfy my request, which pains a horse would scarce have endured. Yet a couple of bells richly contented them.

The Emperor sent his seaman Mantiuas in the evening with bread and victual for me and my men. He, no more scrupulous than the rest, seemed to take a pride in showing how little he regarded that miserable cold and dirty passage, though a dog would scarce have endured it. This kindness I found, when I little expected less than a mischief, but the black night parting our companies, ere midnight the flood served to carry us aboard.

The next day we came ashore, the King with a solemn discourse causing all to depart but his principal men, and this was the effect:

When as he perceived that we had a desire to invade Monacan, against whom he was no professed enemy, yet thus far he would assist us in his enterprise.

First he would send his spies ... to understand their strength and ability to fight, with which he would acquaint us himself. Captain Newport would not be seen in it himself, being great Werowances. They would stay at home. But I, Master Scrivener, and two of his sons, and Opechancanough the King of Pamunkey should have 100 of his men to go before as though they were hunting; they giving us notice where was the advantage, we should kill them. The women and young children he wished we would spare, and bring them to him. Only 100 or 150 of our men he held sufficient for this exploit. Our boats should stay at the falls, where we might hew timber, which we might convey, each man a piece, till we were past the stones; and there join them to pass our men by water. If any were shot, his men should bring them back to our boats.

This fair tale had almost made Captain Newport undertake by this means to discover the South Sea; which will not be without treachery, if we ground our intent upon his constancy.

This day we spent in trading, dancing, and much mirth. The King of Pamunkey sent his messenger (as yet not knowing Captain Newport) to come unto him, who had long expected me, desiring also my father to visit him. The messenger stayed to conduct us, but Powhatan, understanding that we had hatchets lately come from Paspahegh, desired the next day to trade with us, and not to go further. This new trick he cunningly put upon him, but only to have what he listed, and not to try whether we would go or stay.

Opechancanough's messenger returned, that we would not come.

The next day his daughter came to entreat me, showing her father had hurt his leg, and much sorrowed he could not see me.

Captain Newport, being not to be persuaded to go, in that Powhatan had desired us to stay, sent her away with the like answer.

Yet the next day, upon better consideration, enteaty prevailed. And we anchored at Cinquoateck, the first twain above the parting of the river, where dwelled two kings of Pamunkey, brothers to Powhatan; the one called Opitchapam the other Katatough. To these I went ashore, who kindly entreated me and

Master Scrivener, sending some presents aboard to Captain Newport whilst we were trucking with these kings.

Opechancanough, his wife, women, and children came to meet me; with a natural kind affection he seemed to rejoice to see me.

Captain Newport came ashore; with many kind discourses we passed that forenoon. And after dinner, Captain Newport went about with the pinnace to Menapacant, which is twenty miles by water, and not one by land. Opechancanough conducted me and Master Scrivener by land, where, having built a feasting house a purpose to entertain us, with a kind oration, after their manner, and his best provision, kindly welcomed us. That day he would not truck, but did his best to delight us with content.

Captain Newport arrived towards evening, whom the King presented with six great platters of fine bread . . .

The next day till noon we traded. The King feasted all the company, and the afternoon was spent in playing, dancing, and delight. By no means he would have us depart till, the next day, he had feasted us with venison; for which he had sent, having spent his first and second provision in expecting our coming.

The next day he performed his promise, giving more to us three than would have sufficed 30, and in that we carried not away what we left, he sent it after us to the pinnace. With what words or signs of love he could express, we departed.

Captain Newport, in the pinnace, leaving me in the barge to dig a rock, where we supposed a mine, at Cinquoateck; which done, ere midnight, I arrived at Werawocomoco, where our pinnace anchored, being 20 miles from Cinquoateck.

The next day we took leave of Powhatan, who, in regard of his kindness, gave him an Indian. He well affected to go with him for England instead of his son; the cause, I assure me, was to know our strength and country's condition.

The next day we arrived at Kiskiak. The people so scornfully entertained us, as with what signs of scorn and discontent we could, we departed, and returned to our fort with 250 bushels of corn.

Our president, being not wholly recovered of his sickness, in discharging his piece brake and split his hand off, which he is not yet well recovered.

At Captain Newport's arrival, we were victualled for twelve weeks, and having furnished him of what he thought good, he set sail for England the tenth of April. Master Scrivener and myself, with our shallop, accompanied him to Cape Henry, Powhatan having, for a farewell, sent him five or six men's loadings with turkeys, for swords which he sent him in our return to the fort.

We discovered the river of Nansemond, a proud warlike nation, as well we may testify at our first arrival at Chesapeake. But that injury Captain Newport well revenged at his return. Where some of them enticing him to their ambuscadoes by a dance, he, perceiving their intent, with a volley of musket shot slew one, and shot one or two more, as themselves confess. . . .

This is within one day's journey of Chawanoac; the river falleth into the King's River, within twelve miles of Cape Henry.

At our fort, the tools we had were so ordinarily stolen by the Indians, as necessity enforced us to correct their braving the every: for he that stole today, durst come again the next day. One amongst the rest, having stolen two swords, I got the council's consent to set in the bilboes [iron bar with shackles on either end, locked around the ankles]. The next day, with three more, he came, with their wooden swords, in the midst of our men to steal. Their custom is to take anything they can seize off; only the people of Pamunkey we have not found stealing, but what others can steal, their king receiveth. I bade them depart, but flourishing their swords, they seemed to defend what they could catch . . . His pride urged me to turn him from amongst us, whereat he offered to strike me with his sword, which I prevented, striking him first. The rest, offering to revenge the blow, received such an encounter, and fled. The better to afright them, I pursued them with five or six shot, and so chased them out of the island.

The beginner of this broil, little expecting . . . we durst have resisted, having, even till that present, not been contradicted, especially them of Paspahegh: these Indians, within one hour, having by other savages then in the fort understood that I threatened to be revenged, came presently of themselves, and fell to working upon our wares which were then in hand by other savages; who, seeing their pride so encountered, were so submissive, and willing to do any thing as might be, and with trembling fear desired to be friends, within three days after.

From Nansemond, which is 30 miles from us, the King sent us a hatchet which they had stolen from us at our being there . . .

The twenty of April, being at work in hewing down trees and setting corn, an alarum caused us with all speed to take our arms, each expecting a new assault of the savages. But understanding it a boat under sail, our doubts were presently satisfied with the happy sight of Master Nelson . . .

This happy arrival of Master Nelson in the *Phoenix*, having been then about three months missing after Captain Newport's arrival, being to all our expectations lost; albeit that now at the last, having been long crossed with tempestuous weather and contrary winds, his so unexpected coming did so ravish us with exceeding joy that now we thought ourselves as well fitted as our hearts could wish, both with a competent number of men, as also for all other needful provisions, till a further supply should come unto us. . . .

Our next course was to turn husbandmen, to fell trees and set corn. Fifty of our men we employed in this service; the rest kept the fort, to do the command of the president and Captain Martin.

Thirty days the ship lay, expecting the trial of certain matters, which for some cause I keep private.

The next exploit was an Indian, having stolen an axe, was so pursued by Master Scrivener . . . as he threw it down, and, flying, drew his bow at any that durst encounter him.

Within four or five days after, Master Scrivener and I, being a little from the fort, among the corn, two Indians, each with a cudgel, and all newly painted . . . came circling about me as though they would have clubbed me like a hare. I knew their faining love is towards me not without a deadly hatred, but to prevent the worst, I, calling Master Scrivener, retired to the fort.

The Indians, seeing me suspect them, with good terms asked me for some of their men, whom they would beat, and went with me into our fort. Finding one that lay ordinarily with us, only for a spy, they offered to beat him. I, in persuading them to forbear, they offered to begin with me, being now four; for two other, arrayed in like manner, came in on the other side of the fort.

Whereupon I caused to shut the ports, and apprehend them.

The president and council, being presently acquainted, remembering [that] at the first assault they came in like manner . . . concluded to commit them to prison, and expect the event. Eight more we seized at that present.

An hour after came three or four other strangers, extraordinarily fitted with arrows, skins, and shooting gloves. Their jealousy and fear betrayed their bad intent, as also their suspicious departure.

The next day came first an Indian, then another, as ambassadors for their men. They desired to speak with me. Our discourse was that what spades, shovels, swords, or tools they had stolen, to bring home; if not, the next day, they should hang.

The next news was they had taken two of our men ranging in the woods (which mischief no punishment will prevent but hanging), and these they would, should redeem their own 16 or 18; thus braving us to our doors.

We desired the president and Captain Martin, that afternoon to sally upon them, that they might but know what we durst do; and at night, manned our barge, and burned their towns, and spoiled and destroyed what we could.

But they brought our men, and freely delivered them. The president released one. The rest we brought, well guarded, to morning and evening prayers. Our men all in arms, their trembling fear then caused them too much sorrow, which till then scoffed and scorned at what we durst do.

The council concluded that I should terrify them with some torture, to know if I could know their intent.

The next day, I bound one in hold to the main mast, and presenting six muskets with match in the cocks, forced him to desire life. To answer my demands he could not, but one of his comouodos was of the council of Paspahegh, that could satisfy me.

I releasing him out of sight, I affrighted the other, first with the rack, then with muskets; which seeing, he desired me to stay, and he would confess to this execution.

Master Scrivener came; his discourse was to this effect:

That Paspahegh, the Chickahominy, Yaughtawnoone, Pamunkey, Mattapanient, and Kiskiak—these nations were all together a-hunting . . . Paspahegh and Chickahominy had intended to surprise us at work, to have had our tools. Powhatan and all his would seem friends, till Captain Newport's return . . . where, with a great feast, he would so enamor Captain Newport and his men as they should seize on him. And the like traps would be laid for the rest.

This trap . . . we suspected the chief occasion . . . four days before Powhatan had sent the boy he had to us, with many turkeys, to Master Scrivener and me, understanding I would go up unto his countries to destroy them; and he doubted it the more, in that I so oft practised my men, whose shooting he heard to his own lodging, that much feared his wives and children.

We sent him word, we intended no such thing, but only to go to Powhatan to seek stones to make hatchets; except his men shot at us, as Paspahegh had told us they would, which if they did shoot but one arrow, we would destroy them. And, lest this mischief might happen, sent the boy to acquaint him this much, and request him to send us Weanock, one of his subjects, for a guide. . . .

Not long after, Weanock that had been with us for our guide . . . with a false excuse returned; and secretly after him, Amocis the Paspaheghan, who always they kept amongst us for a spy. . . .

The confession of Macanoe, which was the counselor of Paspahegh, first I, then Master Scrivener, upon their several examinations, found by them all confirmed: that Paspahegh and Chickahominy did hate us, and intended some mischief; and who they were that took me; the names of them that stole our tools and swords; and that Powhatan received them, they all agreed. Certain volleys of shot we caused to be discharged, which caused each other to think that their fellows had been slain.

Powhatan, understanding we detained certain savages, sent his daughter, a child of ten years old; which, not only for feature, countenance, and proportion, much exceedeth any of the rest of his people, but for wit and spirit, the only Nonpareil of his country.[8] This he sent by his most trusty messenger, called Rawhunt, as much exceeding in deformity of person, but of a subtle wit and crafty understanding.

He, with a long circumstance, told me how well Powhatan loved and respected me, and in that I should not doubt any way of his kindness, he had sent his child, which he most esteemed, to see me, a deer and bread besides, for a present; desiring me that the boy might come again, which he loved exceedingly. His little daughter he had taught this lesson also, not taking notice at all of the Indians that had been prisoners three days, till that morning that she saw their fathers and friends come quietly, and in good terms to entreat their liberty.

Opechancanough sent also unto us, that for his sake, we would release two that were his friends; and for a token sent me his shooting glove and bracer . . . Now all of them having found their preremptory conditions but to increase our malice, which they, seeing us begin to threaten to destroy them, as familiarly as before, without suspicion or fear, came amongst us, to beg liberty for their men.

In the afternoon, they being gone, we guarded them as before to the church, and after prayer gave them to Pocahontas, the King's daughter, in regard of her father's kindness in sending her. After having well fed them, as all the time of their imprisonment, we gave them their bows, arrows, or what else they had; and with much content, sent them packing. Pocahontas also we requited with such trifles as contented her, to tell that we had used the Paspaheghans very kindly in so releasing them.

The next day we had a suspicion of some other practice for an ambuscado, but perfectly we could not discover it.

Two days after, a Paspaheghan came to show us a glistering mineral stone, and with signs demonstrating it to be in great abundance like unto rocks. With some dozen more, I was sent to seek to dig some quantity, and the Indian to conduct me. But suspecting this some trick to delude us, for to get some copper of us, or with some ambuscado to betray us, seeing him falter in his tale, being two miles on our way, led him ashore. Where abusing us from place to place, and so seeking either to have drawn us with him into the woods, or to have given us the slip, I showed him copper, which I promised to have given him, if he had performed his promise. But for his scoffing and abusing us, I gave him twenty lashes with a rope, and his bows and arrows, bidding him shoot if he durst, and so let him go.

In all this time, our men being all or the most part well recovered, and not willing to trifle away more time then necessity enforced us into, we thought good, for the better content of the adventurers, in some reasonable sort of freight home Master Nelson, with cedar wood. About which, our men going with willing minds, was in very good time effected, and the ship sent for England. We now remaining, being in good health, all our men well contented, free from mutinies, in love one with another, and, as we hope, in a continual peace with the Indians; where we doubt not but by God's gracious assistance, and the adventurers' willing minds and speedy furtherance to so honorable an action, in after times to see our nation to enjoy a country, not only exceeding pleasant habitation, but also very profitable for commerce in general; no doubt pleasing to almighty God, honorable to our gracious sovereign, and commodious generally to the whole kingdom.

Notes

1. Smith, John, *A True Relation of Virginia*, edited with an introduction and notes by Charles Deane (Boston: Wiggin and Lunt, 1866), 7-77

2. Hume, Ivor Noel, *The Virginia Adventure: Roanoke to James Towne, An Archaeological and Historical Odyssey* (Charlottesville: University Press of Virginia, 1994), 127.

3. Rountree, Helen C., *The Powhatan Indians of Virginia* (Norman: University of Oklahoma Press, 1989), 13.

4. Miller, Lee, *Roanoke: Solving the Mystery of the Lost Colony* (New York: Arcade Publishing, 2001), 59, 246-47. According to Miller, Smith misplaced the location of Ocanahonan on a map he drew, which became the map referred to by all subsequent searchers for the Lost Colony. Miller identifies Ocanahonan as Occaneechi Island, which lay in the Roanoke River at the junction of the Staunton and the Dan.

5. This story, of course, has nothing to do with the Jamestown colony's real circumstances; Smith gives no explanation as to why he wants Powhatan to think the English will be leaving soon.

6. Miller, *Roanoke*, 255. Miller translates Anone as Eno, a tribe in central North Carolina.

7. Savage would stay with Powhatan for several years before returning to Jamestown, and will appear in various roles in several narratives.

8. Though not named, the girl referred to here is Pocahontas.

Pocahontas Saves Captain Smith

From

The General History of Virginia, New England, and the Summer Isles by John Smith.[1]

> *Not until Captain John Smith's later writings, published after Pocahontas had become something of a celebrity in England, did Smith bother to describe how the young girl covered his about-to-be-smashed head with her own (by then he was also referring to himself in the third person, as Smith's* General History *was his re-working of others' narratives). Some historians speculate that, if Pocahontas really did rescue Smith as he describes, it was staged, a ritualistic act designed to demonstrate Smith's helplessness and Powhatan's power.[2]*

At last they brought him to Werowocomoco, where was Powhatan their emperor. Here more than two hundred of those grim courtiers stood wondering at him, as he had been a monster; till Powhatan and his train had put themselves in their greatest braveries. Before a fire, upon a seat like a bedstead, he sat covered with a great robe made of rarowcun [raccoon] skins, and all the tails hanging by. On either hand did sit a young wench of 16 or 18 years, and along on each side of the house, two rows of men, and behind them as many women, with all their heads and shoulders painted red; many of their heads bedecked with the white down of birds, but every one with something, and a great chain of white beads about their necks. At his entrance before the king, all the people gave a great shout. The Queen of Appomatoc was appointed to bring him water to wash his hands, and another brought him a bunch of feathers instead of a towel to dry them. Having seated him after their best barbarous manner they could, a long consultation was held, but the conclusion was, two great stones were brought before Powhatan; then as many as could laid hands on him, dragged him to them, and thereon laid his head, and being ready with their clubs to beat out his brains, Pocahontas, the King's dearest daughter, when no entreaty could prevail, got his head in her arms, and laid her own upon his to save him from death. Whereat the Emperor was contented he should live to make him hatchets, and her bells, beads, and copper; for they thought him as well of all occupations as themselves. For the King himself will make his own robes, shoes, bowes, arrows, pots; plant, hunt, or do anything so well as the rest. . . .

<h3 style="text-align:center">NOTES</h3>

1. Smith, John, *The General History of Virginia, New England, and the Summer Isles* (London: Printed by I.D. and I.H. for Michael Sparkes, 1624), 48-49.

2. Hume, Ivor Noel, *The Virginia Adventure: Roanoke to James Towne, An Archaeological and Historical Odyssey*, (Charlottesville: University Press of Virginia, 1994), 178-80.

Captain Smith's Voyage to Pamunkey

From

The General History of Virginia, New England, and the Summer Isles by John Smith.[1]

> *John Smith again encountered Powhatan during a voyage up the Pamunkey River, ostensibly to trade for corn. While this account, taken from Smith's 1624* General History of Virginia, *paints the redoubtable captain's instincts and cunning in a flattering light, it also shows Powhatan to be more than Smith's match as an orator and negotiator. The tale also shows, once again, Pocahontas acting as Smith's savior, apparently betraying her father's designs out of care for the English.*

This company, being victualled but for three or four days, lodged the first night at Warraskoyack, where the President

[Smith] took sufficient provision. This kind king did his best to divert him from seeing Powhatan, but perceiving he could not prevail, he advised in this manner. "Captain Smith, you shall find Powhatan to use you kindly, but trust him not, and be sure he have no opportunity to seize on your arms; for he hath sent for you only to cut your throats." The Captain thanking him for his good counsel; yet the better to try his love, desired guides to Chawanoac, for he would send a present to that king, to bind him his friend. To perform this journey was send Mister Sicklemore, a very valiant, honest, and a painful [painstaking] soldier; with him two guides, and directions how to seek for the lost company of Sir Walter Raleigh, and silk grass. Then we departed thence, the President assuring the King perpetual love, and left with him Samuel Collier his page to learn the language. . . .

The next night being lodged at Kecoughtan; six or seven days the extreme wind, rain, frost, and snow caused us to keep Christmas among the savages, where we were never more merry, nor fed on more plenty of good oysters, fish, flesh, wild fowl, and good bread; nor never had better fires in England, than in the dry smoky houses of Kecoughtan. But departing thence, when we found no houses we were not curious in any weather to lie three or four nights together under the trees by a fire, as formerly is said. A hundred-forty-eight fowls the President, Anthony Bagnall, and Sergeant Pising did kill at three shoots. At Kiskiak the frost and contrary winds forced us three or four days also (to supress the insolency of those proud savages) to quarter in their houses, yet guard our barge, and cause them give us what we wanted; though we were but twelve and himself, yet we never wanted shelter where we found any houses. The 12 of January we arrived at Werowocomoco, where the river was frozen near half a mile from the shore; but to neglect no time, the President with his barge so far had approached by breaking the ice, as the ebb left him amongst those oozy shoals, yet rather than to lie there froze to death, by his own example he taught them to march near middle deep, a flight shot through this muddy frozen ooze. When the barge floated, he appointed two or three to return her aboard the pinnace. Where for want of water in melting the ice, they made fresh water, for the river there was salt. But in this march Mister Russell (whom none could persuade to stay behind), being somewhat ill, and exceeding heavy, so overtoiled himself as the rest had much ado (ere he got ashore) to regain life into his dead, benumbed spirits. Quartering in the next houses we found, we sent to Powhatan for provision, who sent us plenty of bread, turkeys, and venison; the next day having seated us after his ordinary manner, he began to ask us when we would be gone, faining he sent not for us, neither had he any corn, and his people much less, yet for forty swords he would procure us forty baskets. The President showing him the men there present that brought him the message and conditions, asked Powhatan how it chanced he became so forgetful; thereat the King concluded the matter with a merry laughter, asking for our commodities, but none he liked without guns and swords, valuing a basket of corn more precious than a basket of copper, saying he could eat his corn, but not the copper.

Captain Smith seeing the intent of this subtle savage began to deal with him after this manner. "Powhatan, though I had many courses to have made my provision, yet believing your promises to supply my wants, I neglected all to satisfy your desire, and to testify my love, I sent you my men for your building, neglecting mine own.[2] What your people had you have engrossed, forbidding them our trade; and now you think by consuming the time, we shall consume for want, not having to fulfill your strange demands. As for swords and guns, I told you long ago I had none to spare, and you must know those I have can keep me from want; yet steal or wrong you I will not, nor dissolve that friendship we have mutually promised, except you constrain me by our bad usage."

The King, having attentively listened to this discourse, promised that both he and his country would spare him what he could, the which within two days they should receive. "Yet Captain Smith," sayeth the King, "some doubt I have of your coming hither, that makes me not so kindly seek to relieve you as I would; for many do inform me, your coming hither is not for trade, but to invade my people, and possess my country, who dare not come to bring you corn, seeing you thus armed with your men. To free us of this fear, leave aboard your weapons, for here they are needless, we being all friends, and forever Powhatans."

With many such discourses they spent the day, quartering that night in the King's houses. The next day he renewed his building, which he little intended should proceed. For the Dutchmen finding his plenty, and knowing our want, and perceiving his preparations to surprise us, little thinking we could escape both him and famine, (to obtain his favor) revealed to him so much as they knew of our estates and projects, and how to prevent them. One of them being of so great a spirit, judgement, and resolution, and a hireling that was certain of his wages for his labor, and ever well used both he and his countrymen, that the President knew not whom better to trust, and not knowing any fitter for that employment, had sent him as a spy to discover Powhatan's intent, then little doubting his honesty, nor could ever be certain of his villainy till near half a year after.

Whilst we expected the coming in of the country, we wrangled out of the King ten quarters of corn for a copper kettle, the which the President perceiving him much to affect, valued it at a much greater rate; but in regard of his scarcity he would accept it, provided we should have as much more the next year, or else the country of Monacan. Wherewith each seemed well contented, and Powhatan began to expostulate the difference of peace and war after this manner.

"Captain Smith, you may understand that I having seen the death of all my people thrice, and not anyone living of those three generations but myself; I know the difference of peace and war better than any in my country. But now I am old and ere long must die, my brethren, namely Opitchapam, Opechancanough, and Katatough, my two sisters, and their two daughters, are distinctly each others' successors. I wish their experience no less than mine, and your love to them no less than mine to you. But this bruit [rumor, report] from Nansemond, that you are come to destroy my country, so much affrighteth all my people as they dare not visit you. What will it avail you to take by force you may quickly have by love, or to destroy them that provide you food? What can you get by war, when we can hide our provisions and fly to the woods? Whereby you must famish by wronging us your friends. And why are you thus jealous of our loves seeing us unarmed, and both do, and are willing still to feed you, with that you cannot get but by our labors? Think you I am so simple, not to know it is better to eat good meat, lie well, and sleep quietly with my women and children, laugh and be merry with you, have copper, hatchets, or what I want being your friend, than be forced to fly from all, to lie cold in the woods, feed upon acorns, roots, and such trash, and be so hunted by you, that I can neither rest, eat, nor sleep, but my tired men must watch, and if a twig but break, everyone cryeth there cometh Captain Smith. Then must I fly I know not whither, and thus with miserable fear, end my miserable life, leaving my pleasures to such youths as you, which through your rash unadvisedness may quickly as miserably end, for want of that, you never know where to find. Let this therefore assure you of our loves, and every year our friendly trade shall furnish you with corn; and now also, if you would come in friendly manner to see us, and not thus with your guns and swords as to invade your foes." To this subtle discourse, the President thus replied.

"Seeing you will not rightly conceive of our words, we strive to make you know our thoughts by our deeds; the vow I made you of my love, both myself and my men have kept. As for your promise I find it every day violated by some of your subjects; yet we finding your love and kindness, our custom is so far from being ungrateful, that for your sake only, we have curbed our thirsting desire of revenge, else had they known as well the cruelty we use to our enemies, as our true love and courtesy to our friends. And I think your judgement sufficient to conceive, as well by the adventures we have undertaken, as by the advantage we have (by our arms) of yours, that had we intended you any hurt, long ere this we could have affected it. Your people coming to James Towne are entertained with their bows and arrows without any exceptions; we esteeming it with you as it is with us, to wear our arms as our apparel. As for the danger of our enemies, in such wars consist our chiefest pleasure. For your riches we have no use. As for the hiding your provision, or by your flying to the woods, we shall not so unadvisedly starve as you conclude, your friendly care in that behalf is needless, for we have a rule to find beyond your knowledge."

Many other discourses they had, till at last they began to trade. But the King, seeing his will would not be admitted as a law, our guard dispersed, nor our men disarmed, he (sighing) breathed his mind once more in this manner.

"Captain Smith, I never use any werowance so kindly as yourself, yet from you I receive the least kindness of any. Captain Newport gave me swords, copper, clothes, a bed, towels, or what I desired; ever taking what I offered him, and would send away his guns when I entreated him. None doth deny to lie at my feet, or refuse to do what I desire, but only you, of whom I can have nothing but what you regard not, and yet you will have whatsoever you demand. Captain Newport you call father, and so you call me, but I see for all us both you will do what you list, and we must both seek to content you. But if you intend so friendly as you say, send hence your arms, that I may believe you; for you see the love I bear you doth cause me thus nakedly to forget myself."

Smith, seeing this savage but trifle the time to cut his throat, procured the savages to break the ice, that his boat might come to fetch his corn and him, and gave order for more men to come on shore, to surprise the King, with whom also he but trifled the time till his men were landed, and to keep him from suspicion, entertained the time with this reply.

"Powhatan you must know, as I have but one God, I honor but one king; and I live here not as your subject, but as your friend to pleasure you with what I can. By the gifts you bestow on me, you gain more than by trade; yet would you visit me as I do you, you should know it is not our custom to sell our courtesies as a vendable commodity. Bring all your country with you for your guard, I will not dislike it as being over jealous. But to content you, tomorrow I will leave my arms, and trust to your promise. I call you father indeed, and as a father you shall see I will love you; but the small care you have of such a child caused my men to persuade me to look to myself."

By this time Powhatan having knowledge his men were ready whilst the ice was breaking, with his luggage, women, and children, fled. Yet to avoid suspicion, left two or three of the women talking with the Captain, whilst he secretly ran away, and his men . . . secretly beset the house. Which being presently discovered to Captain Smith, with his pistol, sword, and target he made such a passage among these naked devils that at the first shot, they next him tumbled one over another, and the rest quickly fled some one way some another. So that without any hurt, only accompanied with John Russell, he obtained the corps de guard. When they perceived him so well escaped, and with his eighteen men (for he had no more with him ashore) to the uttermost of their skill they sought excuses to dissemble the matter; and Powhatan to excuse his flight and the sudden coming of this multitude sent our Captain a great bracelet and a chain of pearl, by an ancient orator that bespoke us to this purpose, perceiving even then from our pinnace, a barge and men departing and coming unto us.

"Captain Smith, our werowance is fled, fearing your guns, and knowing when the ice was broken there would come more men, sent these numbers but to guard his corn from stealing that might happen without your knowledge. Now, though some be hurt by your misprision, yet Powhatan is your friend and so will ever continue. Now since the ice is open, he would have you send away your corn, and if you would have his company, send away also your guns, which so affrighteth his people, that they dare not come to you as he promised they should."

Then having provided baskets for our men to carry our corn to the boats, they kindly offered their service to guard our arms, that none should steal them. A great many they were, of goodly well proportioned fellows, as grim as devils; yet the very sight of cocking our matches, and being to let fly, a few words caused them to leave their bows and arrows to our guard, and bear down our corn on their backs; we needed not importune them to make dispatch. But our barges being left on the ooze by the ebb caused us stay till the next high water, so that we returned again to our old quarter. Powhatan and his Dutchmen bursting with desire to have the head of Captain Smith, for if they could but kill him, they thought all was theirs, neglected not any opportunity to effect this purpose. The Indians with all the merry sports they could devise spent the time till night; then they all returned to Powhatan, who all this time was making ready his forces to surprise the house and him at supper. Notwithstanding, the eternal all-seeing God did prevent him, and by a strange means. For Pocahontas his dearest jewel and daughter, in that dark night came through the irksome woods, and told our Captain great cheer should be sent us by and by; but Powhatan and all the power he could make would after come kill us all, if they that brought it could not kill us with our own weapons when we were at supper. Therefore if we would live she wished us presently to be gone. Such things as she delighted in, he would have given her; but with the tears running down her cheeks, she said she durst not be seen to have any, for if Powhatan should know it, she were but dead, and so she ran away by herself as she came. Within less than an hour came eight or ten lusty fellows, with great platters of venison and other victual, very importunate to have us put out our matches (whose smoke made them sick) and sit down to our victual. But the Captain made them taste every dish, which done he sent some of them back to Powhatan, to bid him make haste for he was prepared for his coming. As for them he knew they came to betray him at his supper, but he would prevent them and all their other intended villainies, so that they might be gone. Not long after came more messengers, to see what news; not long after them, others. Thus we spent the night as vigilantly as they, till it was high water, yet seemed to the savages as friendly as they to us; and that we were so desirous to give Powhatan content, as he requested, we did leave him Edward Brynton to kill him fowl, and the Dutchmen to finish his house, thinking at our return from Pamunkey the frost would be gone, and then we might find a better opportunity if necessity did occasion it, little dreaming yet of the Dutchmen's treachery.

NOTES

1. Smith, John, *The General History of Virginia, New England, and the Summer Isles* (London: Printed by I.D. and I.H. for Michael Sparkes, 1624), 74-78.

2. Hume, Ivor Noel, *The Virginia Adventure: Roanoke to James Towne, An Archaeological and Historical Odyssey* (Charlottesville: University Press of Virginia, 1994), 223. One of Powhatan's requests, in exchange for corn, was a house such as those where the English resided in Jamestown. Smith sent him six men to build it; four of these were the "Dutchmen"— Germans or *Deutschmenn* actually—to whom the narrative refers.

PART III

The Starving Time

1609-1610

"Unnecessary Inmates"

From
A letter from the council and company of the honorable plantation in Virginia to the Lord Mayor, Aldermen, and Companies of London[1]

Once a foothold, however tenuous, had been established, the Council of the Virginia Company in London took the steps they thought necessary to turn Jamestown from an outpost into a going concern.

Much has been made about early Virginia being top-heavy with nobles and gentlemen, at the expense of the farmers and laborers who could have kept the colonists sufficiently fed and sheltered. Ivor Noel Hume in The Virginia Adventure *points out that this is a misconception: not only were most of the commoners not named on the passenger rolls, and have therefore been overlooked by historians examining the makeup of the colony, but many of the colonists listed as gentlemen had only recently earned that legal distinction, and probably lacked the refined sensibilities (and manual incompetence) that we associate with the term.[2]*

Another common assumption about the bulk of Jamestown's colonists is that they were the wretched of English society, dumped upon the American wilderness. Documents such as this letter from the Council of Virginia do little to prove that assumption wrong. Roughly four out of every five colonists sent to Virginia died of disease, starvation, or Indian attack. Though Jamestown's first two women arrived with the Second Supply in 1608, only one of them was unmarried (not for long), and if Jamestown was going to stay populated it needed a steady stream of immigrants, whether they came from the depths of Newgate Prison or not. To the Council of Virginia, their proposal to the Lord Mayor of London was completely sensible and mutually beneficial.

Whereas the lords of his Majesty's council, commissioners for the subsidy, desirest to ease the city and suburbs of a swarm of unnecessary inmates, as a continual cause of dearth and famine, and the very original cause of all the plagues that happened in this kingdom, have advised your lordship and your brethren in a case of state, to make some voluntary contribution for their remove into this plantation of Virginia, which we understand you all seemeth to like as an action pleasing to God and happy for this commonwealth.

We the council and company of this honorable plantation willing to yield unto your Lordship and them all good satisfaction, have entered into consultation with ourselves what may be the charge of every private man and what every private family, which we send herewith at large, not as a thing which we seek to exact from you, but that you may see, as in a true glass, the precise charge, which we wholly commend to your grave wisdom, both for the sum and manner of levy: only give us leave thus far to inform you that we give no bills of adventure for a less sum than 12 [pounds], 10 [shillings], presuming it would breed an infinite trouble now and a confusion in the contribution. But if your Lordship make any easement or raise any voluntary contribution from the best disposed and most able of the companies, we are willing to give our bills of adventure to the masters and wardens to the general use and behoof of that company. If by wards to the alderman and his deputy, to the perpetual good of that ward, or otherwise, as it shall please you and your brethren out of your better experience to direct. And if the inmate called before you and enjoined to remove shall allege that he hath not place to remove unto, but must lie in the streets; and being offered to go this journey, shall demand what may be their present maintenance, what may be their future hopes? It may please you to let them know that for the present they shall have meat, drink and clothing, with a house, orchard and garden, for the meanest family, and a possession of land to them and their posterity, 100 acres for every man's person that hath a trade, or a body able to endure day labor, as much for his wife, as much for his child, that are of years to do service to the colony, with further particular award according to their particular merits and industry.

And if your lordship and your brethren shall be pleased to put in any private adventures for yourselves in particular, you shall be sure to receive according to the proportion of the adventure, equal part with us adventurers from the beginning, both of the commodities returned and of the lands to be divided.

And because you shall see, being aldermen of so famous a city, we give you due respect, we are contented, having but one badge of grace and favor from his Majesty to participate with you therein and to make as many of you as shall adventure, 50 or more, fellow councilors from the first day with us who have spent double and treble as much as is required, abiding the hazard of three several discoveries with much care and diligence and many days attendance.

And as your deputies are your assistants in your private wards so shall as many of them as will adventure but 25 present money, be made partners of this company and assistants of this council.

And thus, as an action concerning God, and the advancement of religion, the present ease, future honor and safety of the kingdom, the strength of our navy, the visible hope of a great and rich trade, and many secret blessings not yet discovered, we wholly commend the cause to the wisdom and zeal of your self and your brethren, and you and it, and us all to the holy protection of the almighty.

NOTES

1. Brown, Alexander, *Genesis of the United States* (Cambridge: The Riverside Press, 1890), 252-53.

2. Hume, Ivor Noel, *The Virginia Adventure: Roanoke to James Towne, An Archaeological and Historical Odyssey* (Charlottesville: University Press of Virginia, 1994), 121-22.

Nova Britannia

From
Nova Britannia: Offering Most Excellent fruits by Planting in Virginia, Exciting all such as be well affected to further the same.[1]

> Nova Britannia *is a piece of the purest propaganda, a pamphlet representing the finest in seventeenth-century marketing techniques. Its author is assumed to be one Robert Johnson, acting as a one-man public relations department for the Virginia Company, and its purpose was to recruit new investors. In addition to describing the natural bounty to be found in Virginia (so what if there is no gold?), and dismissing the reports of famine and disease that had already crossed the Atlantic (oh, that was all the old colonists' fault),* Nova Britannia *invokes the example of Elizabeth and her "sea dogs,"*

seeking to shame its readers into undertaking or undersigning this patriotic (if more than a little risky) expedition.

To the Right Worshipful Sir Thomas Smith, of London, Knight of one of his Majesty's Council for Virginia, and Treasurer for the Colony, and Governor of the Companies of the Moscovia and East India Merchants, peace, health, and happiness in Christ.

Right worshipful Sir,

Forasmuch as I have always observed your honest zeal to God, accompanied with so excellent carriage and resolution in actions of best consequence, I cannot but discover unto you, for your further encouragement, the sum of a private speech or discourse, touching our plantation in Virginia, uttered not long since in London, where some few adventurers (well affecting the enterprise) being met together touching their intended project, one among the rest stood up and began to relate (in effect) as followeth.

R. J.

. . . There are divers monuments already published in print to the world, manifesting and showing that the coasts and parts of Virginia have been long since discovered, peopled, and possessed by many English, both men, women, and children, the natural subjects of our late Queen Elizabeth, of famous memory, conducted and left there at sundry times. And that the same footing and possession is there kept and possessed by the same English, or by their seed and offspring, without any interruption or invasion, either of the savages (the natives of the country) or of any other prince or people (for ought we hear or know) to this day, which argueth sufficiently to us (and it is true) that over those English and Indian people, no Christian King or Prince (other then James our sovereign Lord and King) ought to have rule or dominion, or can, by possession, conquest, or inheritance, truly claim or make just title to those territories, or to any part thereof, except it be (as we hear of late) that a challenge is laid to all, by virtue of a donation from Alexander the first Pope of Rome, wherein (they say) is given all the West Indies, including Florida and Virginia, with all America, and whatsoever islands adjacent.[2]

But what is this to us? They are blind indeed that stumble here; it is much like that great donation of Constantine whereby the Pope himself doth hold and claim the city of Rome and all the Western Empire, a thing that so crosseth all histories of truth, and sound antiquity, that by the apt resemblance of those two donations, the whole West Empire, from a temporal Prince to the Pope, and the whole West Indies, from the Pope to a temporal Prince. I do verily guess they be near of kin, they are so like each other, the one an old tale, vain and fabulous, the other a new toy, most idle and ridiculous.

Letting go, therefore, these legendary fables, which howsoever some men hold authentic as their creed, yet are they, in the judgment of wise men, things of no value, nor do import to us any cause of doubt or fear, but that we go on in our honest enterprise, and lawful purpose now in hand, that (as we hope) his Majesty mindeth not the relinquishing his estate and interest, derived to him by right of succession from his immediate predecessor, but for the further planting and succouring our old colony, hath given us leave to make new supplies, which we lately sent thither under the conduct of Christopher Newport, Captain;

and hath granted many gracious privileges, under the great seal, to us and to our heirs forever, that will adventure or plant in the said plantation. So I wish and entreat all well affected subjects, some in their persons, others in their purses, cheerfully to adventure, and jointly take in hand this high and acceptable work, tending to advance and spread the kingdom of God, and the knowledge of the truth, among so many millions of men and women, savage and blind, that never yet saw the true light shine before their eyes, to enlighten their minds and comfort their souls, as also for the honor of our King, and enlarging of his kingdom, and for preservation and defence of that small number our friends and countrymen already planted, lest for want of more supplies we become a scorn to the world, subjecting our former adventurers to apparent spoil and hazard, and our people (as a prey) to be sacked and pulled out of possession . . . and which is the least and last respect (yet usually preferred), for the singular good and benefit that will undoubtedly arise to this whole nation, and to every one of us in particular that will adventure therein, as by true relation (God willing) I shall make it manifestly appear to all.

It is known to the world, and cannot be forgotten, that the days and reign of Queen Elizabeth brought forth the highest degree of wealth, happiness, and honor that ever England had before her time, whereof to let pass the particular praises, as impertinent to my purpose, I do only call to mind our royal fleets and merchants' ships . . . our excellent navigators, and admirable voyages, as into all parts and round about the globe with good success, to the high fame and glory of our nation. So especially their aim and course was most directed to the new found world, to the mainland and infinite islands of the West Indies, intending to discover with what convenience to plant and settle English colonies in places not already possessed and inhabited by subjects of other Christian princes. . . .

But seeing we so passed by their dwellings, that in seating ourselves, we sought not to unsettle them, but by God's mercy, after many storms, were brought to the coast of another country, far distant and remote from their habitations. Why should any frown or envy at it; or if they do, why should we (neglecting so fair an opportunity) faint or fear to enlarge ourselves? Where is our force and ancient vigor? Doth our late reputation sleep in the dust? No, no, let not the world deceive itself; we still remain the same, and upon just occasion given, we shall quickly show it too. Having now, by God's blessing, more means than ever heretofore, being strongly fenced where we wonted to lie open, our plant, we trust, is firmly rooted, our arms and limbs are strong, our branches fair, and much desire to spread themselves abroad.

But before I come to describe this earthly paradise, or to prove the points of my proposition mentioned before, you shall know that the first discovery and actual possession taken thereof was in the reign and by the subjects of Henry the seventh of England, at which time did Spain also discover, and by that right of discovery, doth retain and hold their Nova Hispania, and all other their limits upon that coast.[3] But that we now intend to ground upon is a more late discovery and actual possession, taken in the name and right of Queen Elizabeth, in Anno 1584, the 13th of July, as it is truly set down in the *Book of English Voyages, by sundry English Captains and Gentlemen in that Voyage*, whose names are recorded in that discourse (and many of which are yet living) whereof when her Majesty had true information, she named the country Virginia, and did assign to Walter Raleigh (then a gentleman of worth) power and authority to plant forces and colonies there, at his pleasure, who transported thither in Anno 1587, by the conduct of John White, chief leader, above a hundred men, women, and children at one time, and left them there to inhabit to this day.[4] Notwithstanding, it is true indeed (as some may object). It is now above twenty years ago since these things were done, and yet ever since in all this time, we never saw or heard of any good that hath come from thence, nor of any hope, that might encourage us anew to engage ourselves therein.

But let us rightly weigh the reasons of it, and then judge. Those hundred and upwards, conducted thither by John White, and whose particular names you may see recorded in the same *Book of Voyages*, were left there, with intent and promise, to be supplied from England, with more companies and all necessaries, the next year following. In the meantime, they were to plant and fortify themselves in best manner they could, and to make a discovery of such minerals, and other merchandise, as the country should yield by nature. But as all good actions have their crosses and their bane attending on them, so had this; for that those which had the managing of a new supply, being the next year sufficiently furnished to sea for that end, yet most unnaturally, being tainted with that common corruption of time, turned their head another way, and with greedy minds, betook themselves wholly to hunt after pillage upon the Spanish coast, where, spending their men, their time and provisions, they were not able (being come and arrived at the port) to make up into the land to visit and relieve their friends, but were forced to retire for England again, whereby the edge of those adventurers that set them forth was so abated, that this most honorable enterprise, so happily begun, was by this last occasion most unhappily ended.[5] Neither had our poor countrymen left there any means from thence to visit us, nor in all this time to give us any light of their own estate. Whereas then, if those beginnings had been followed as they ought, and as by God's help we now intend, that country had long since become a most royal addition to the Crown of England, and a very nursery and fountain of much wealth and strength to this kingdom. . . .

And this I but mention to note the blind diffidence of our English natures, which laugh to scorn the name of Virginia, and all other new projects, be they never so probable, and will not believe till we see the effects; as also to show how capable men ought to be, in things of great importance, advisedly to take the first occasions. We read of Hannibal, when chasing home the Romans to the gates of Rome, and neglecting then to scale the walls, could never after, with all his strength and policies, come near the like advantage. Yet I must briefly tell you now, what I conceive with joy, that howsoever the business of this plantation hath been formerly miscarried, yet it is now going on in better way, not enterprised by one or two private subjects, who in their greatness of mind sought to compass that which rather beseemed a mighty prince (such as ours) or the whole state to take in hand. For it is not unknown to you all how many noble men of honorable minds, how many worthy knights, merchants, and others of the best disposition, are now joined together in one charter, to receive equal privileges, according to their several adventures: every man engaging his purse, and some noblemen, knights, and gentlemen intending to go in their own persons, which I did hear to protest and vow against any people whomsoever shall any way seek to entrap or impeach our proceedings, and utter revenge upon their bodies or goods, if they be to be found upon sea or land. Whereby we have assured hope (God assisting us) to be effectually able to make good against all, and in short time to bring to a most happy event the thing we take in hand.

And now in describing the natural seat and disposition of the country itself. . . . First, the voyage is not long nor tedious; six weeks at ease will send us thither, whereas six months suffice not to some other places where we trade. Our course and passage is through the great ocean, where is no fear of rocks or flats, nor subject to the straits and restraint of foreign princes. Most winds that blow are apt and fit for us, and none can hinder us. When we come to the coast there is continual depth enough, with good bottom for anchor hold, and the land is fair to fall with all, full of excellent good harbors. The world affords no better for ships of all burdens, many pleasant islands great and small affronting the coast. Two goodly rivers are discovered winding far into the main, the one in the north part of the land by our Western Colony, Knights and Gentlemen of Exeter, Plymouth, and others; the other in the South part thereof by our Colony of London, upon which river, being both broad, deep, and pleasant, abounding with store of fish, our colony have begun to fortify themselves, and have built a town, and named it (in honor of our King) James Towne, fourscore miles within land, upon the north side of the river (as is London upon the River of Thames). From whence we have discovered the same river one hundred miles further into the mainland, in the searching whereof they were so ravished with the admirable sweetness of the stream, and with the pleasant land trending along on either side, that their joy exceeded, and with great admiration they praised God.

The country itself is large and great assuredly, though as yet no exact discovery can be made of all. It is also commendable and hopeful every way, the air and climate most sweet and wholesome, much warmer than England, and very agreeable to our natures. It is inhabited with wild and savage people that live and lie up and down in troops like herds of deer in a forest. They have no law but nature, their apparel skins of beasts, but most go naked. The better sort have houses, but poor ones. They have no arts nor science, yet they live under superior command, such as it is. They are generally very loving and gentle, and do entertain and relieve our people with great kindness. They are easy to be brought to good, and would fain embrace a better condition. The land yieldeth naturally for the sustentation of man, abundance of fish, both scale and shell; of land and water fowls, infinite store of deer, kine and fallow, stags, coneys, and hares, with many fruits and roots good for meat. . . .

For the first (if I forget not myself) how it may tend to advance the kingdom of God, by reducing savage people from their blind superstition to the light of religion, when some object, we seek nothing less than the cause of God, being led on by our own private ends, and secondly how we can warrant a supplantation of those Indians, or an invasion into their right and possessions.

To the first we say, as many actions, both good in themselves, and in their success, have been performed with bad intents: so in this case, howsoever our naughtiness of mind may sway very much, yet God may have the honor, and his kingdom advanced in the action done. But yet, by the way, me thinks this objection comes in due time, and doth well admonish us, how to rectify our hearts and ground our meditations before we begin. We do generally applaud, and highly commend, the goodness of the cause, and that it is such a profitable plow, as every honest man ought to set his hand unto, both in respect of God and the public good. This is our general voice, and we say truth, for so it is.

But we must beware that under this pretense that bitter root of greedy gain be not so settled in our hearts that, being in a golden dream, if it fall not out presently to our expectation, we slink away with discontent, and draw our purses from the charge. If any show this affection, I would wish his baseness of mind to be noted. What must be our direction, then, no more but this: if thou dost once approve the work, lay thy hand to it cheerfully, and withdraw it not till thy task be done. At all assays and new supplies of money be not lag, nor like a dull horse that's always in the lash, for here lies the poison of all good attempts. . . . But are we to look for no gain in the lieu of all adventures? Yes, undoubtedly, there is assured hope of gain, as I will show anon in due place, but look it be not chief in your thoughts. . . . And as for supplanting the savages, we have no such intent. Our intrusion into their possessions shall tend to their great good, and no way to their hurt, unless as unbridled beasts they procure it to themselves. . . .

But for my second point propounded, the honor of our King, by enlarging his kingdoms, to prove how this may tend to that. No argument of mine can make it so manifest as the same is clear in itself. Divine testimonies show that the honor of a king consisteth in the multitude of subjects. . . . Honorable I grant is just conquest by sword, and Hercules is fained to have had all his felicity in subduing and rooting out the tyrants of the world, but unfainedly, it is most honorable indeed to subdue the tyranny of the roaring lion, that devours those poor souls in their ignorance, and leads them to hell for want of light. When our dominions shall be enlarged, and the subjects multiplied of a people so bought and ransomed, not by storms of raging cruelties (as West India was converted) with rapier's point and musket shot, murdering so many millions of naked Indians, as their stories do relate, but by fair and loving means, suiting to our English natures. . . .

And as for the third part, the relieving our men already planted, to preserve both them and our former adventures, I shall not need to say much, the necessity is so apparent that I hope no adventurer will be wanting therein. . . .

And now it follows, how it can be good for this commonwealth, which is likewise most apparent many ways. First, if we consider what strength of shipping may be raised and maintained thence, in furnishing our own wants of sundry kinds, and the wants of other nations, too, in such needful things arising thence which can hardly now be obtained from any other part of the world, as plank and timber for shipping. . . . And from thence we may have iron and copper also in great quantity, about which the expense and waste of wood, as also for building of ships, will be no hurt, but great service to that country; the great superfluity whereof, the continual cutting down, in many hundred years, will not be able to overcome, whereby will likewise grow a greater benefit to this land, in preserving our woods and timber at home, so infinitely and without measure, upon these occasions cut down, and fallen to such a sickness and wasting consumption, as all the physic in England cannot cure.

We doubt not but to make there, in few years, store of good wines, as any from the Canaries, by replanting and making tame the vines that naturally grow there in great abundance. Only send men of skill to do it, and coopers to make casks, and hoops for that and all other uses, for which there is wood enough at hand. . . .

For as I told you before, there must be art and industry with our helps and means extended, with a little patience to bring these things to pass. We must not look to reap with joy, except we sow in tears. The abundance of King Solomon's gold and silver did not rain from heaven upon the heads of his subjects, but heavenly providence blessed his navigations and public affairs, the chief means of their wealth. . . .

And now to our present business in hand, which so many stumble at, in regard of the continual charge. I would have them know that it cannot be great nor long, as the business may be handled. Two things are especially required herein: people to make the plantation, and money to furnish our present provisions and shipping now in hand. For the first we need not doubt, our land abounding with swarms of idle persons, which, having no means of labor to relieve their misery, do likewise swarm in lewd and naughty practices, so that if we seek not some ways for their foreign employment, we must provide shortly more prisons and corrections for their bad conditions. . . .

Yet I do not mean that none but such unsound members, and such poor as want their bread, are fittest for this employment; for we intend to have of every trade and profession, both honest, wise and painful men, whereof our land and city is able to spare and furnish many (as we had experience in our last sending thither) which will be glad to go and plant themselves so happily, and their children after them, to hold and keep conformity with the laws, language, and religion of England for ever.

Touching which, I do earnestly admonish you to beware and shun three kinds of people: the first, a most vile minded sort, and for the most part bad members of this city, by some means shaken out of their honest courses, and now shifting by their wits, will be always devising some unhappiness to wrong the plantation . . . and would (if they were not met withal and curbed by authority) make a monopoly to themselves, of each thing after other, belonging to the freedom of every man's profession, the very wrack of merchandising.

The second sort are papists, professed or recusant, of which I would not one, seasoned with the least taint of that leaven, to be settled in our plantation, nor in any part of that country; but if once perceived such a one, weed him out, and ship him home for England, for they will ever be plotting and conspiring to root you out if they can. Howsoever they swear, flatter, and equivocate, believe them not. . . .

The third sort to avoid are evil-affected magistrates, a plague that God himself complains of. . . . But in men of knowledge and religious education, there is ever found true humility, temperance, and justice, joined with confidence, valor, and noble courage. . . . Ten of such will chase a hundred. No adversity can make them despair; their provident care will ever be to repulse injuries, and repress the insolent; to encourage the painful and best minded; to employ the soul to some honest labors; and to relieve, with mercy and commiseration, the most feeble, weakest, and meanest member.

And as for the general sort that shall go to be planters, be they never so poor, so they be honest, and painful, the place will make them rich. All kind of artificers we must first employ . . . carpenters, shipwrights, masons, sawyers, brickmakers, bricklayers, plowmen, sowers, planters, fishermen, coopers, smiths, metalmen, tailers, turners, and such like, to make and fit all necessaries for comfort and use of the colony. And for such as are of no trades (if they be industrious) they shall have there employment enough, for there is a world of means to set many thousands a-work, partly in such things as I mentioned before, and many other profitable works, for no man must live idle there. . . .

We intend to plant there (God willing) great plenty of sugar canes, for which the soil and climate is very apt and fit; also linseed and rapeseeds to make oils, which, because the soil is strong and cheap, may there be sowed and the oil made to great benefit. We must plant also oranges, lemons, almonds, aniseeds, rices, cumin, cotton wool, carroway seeds, ginger, madder, olives, oris, sumac, and many such like, which I cannot now name; all very good merchandise, and will there grow and increase, as well as in Italy or any other part of the straits, whence we fetch them now. And in searching the land there is undoubted hope of finding cochinell, the plant of rich indigo, grainberries, beaver hides, pearls, rich treasure, and the South Sea, leading to China, with many other benefits which our daylight will discover.

But of all other things that God hath denied that country, there is want of sheep to make woollen cloth; and this want of cloth must always be supplied from England, whereby, when the colony is thoroughly increased, and the Indians brought to our civility (as they will in short time), it will cause a mighty vent of English clothes, a great benefit to our nation, and raising again of that ancient trade of clothing, so much decayed in England. . . .

The second thing to make this plantation is money, to be raised among the adventurers, wherein the sooner and more deeply men engage themselves, their charge will be the shorter, and their gain the greater, as in this last point which I have to speak for the good of each particular adventurer, I will make it plain.

First, you shall understand that his Majesty hath granted us an enlargement of our charter, with many ample privileges, wherein we have knights and gentlemen of good place named for the King's council of Virginia to govern us, as also every planter and adventurer shall be inserted in the patent by name. This ground being laid, we purpose presently to make supply of men, women and children (so many as we can) to make the plantation. We call those planters that go in their persons to dwell there, and those adventurers that adventure their money and go not in person, and both do make the members of one colony. We do account twelve pound, ten shillings, to be a single share adventured. Every ordinary man or woman, if they will go and dwell there, and every child above ten years that shall be carried thither to remain, shall be allowed for each of their persons a single share, as if they had adventured twelve pound, ten shillings in money. Every extraordinary man, as divines, governors, ministers of state and justice, knights, gentlemen, physicians, and such as be men of worth for special services, are all to go as planters, and to execute their several functions in the colony, and are to be maintained at the common charge, and are to receive their dividend (as others do) at seven years' end. And they are to be agreed with all before they go, and to be rated by the council according to the value of their persons, which shall be set down and registered in a book, that it may always appear what people have gone to the plantation, at what time they went, and how their persons were valued. And likewise, if any that go to be planters will lay down money to the treasurer, it shall be also registered and their shares enlarged accordingly, be it for more or less. All charges of settling and maintaining the plantation, and of making supplies, shall be born in a joint stock of the adventurers for seven years after the date of our new enlargement; during which time, there shall be no adventure, nor goods returned in private from thence, neither by master, mariner, planter, nor passenger. They shall be restrained by bond and search, that as we supply from hence to the planters at our own charge all necessaries for food and apparel, for fortifying and building of houses in a joint stock, so they are also to return from thence the increase and fruits of their labors for the use and advancement of the same joint stock till the end of seven years. At which time, we purpose (God willing) to make a division by commissioners appointed of all the lands granted unto us by his Majesty, to every of the colony, according to each man's several adventure, agreeing with our register book, which we doubt not will be for every share of twelve pound, ten shillings, five hundred acres at least. Now if any think that we shall be tied to a continual charge of making new supplies for seven years, let them conceive thus much, that if we do it thoroughly at the first, by engaging ourselves at once in furnishing many men and other means, assuredly after the second year the returns from thence will be able, with an over-plus, to make supplies at large, so that our purses shall be freed. And the over-plus of stock will also grow to greatness, which stock is also (as the land) to be divided equally at seven years' end or sooner, or so often as the company shall think fit, for the greatness of it, to make a dividend. . . .

Whereby, undoubtedly, we shall be soon freed from further expence, our gains will grow, and our stock increase; we shall fell our timber, saw our plank, and quickly make good shipping there, and shall return from thence, with good employment, a hundred sail of good ships yearly. All which good, and much more, we shall withstand and bring ourselves into a labyrinth, if we pinch and spare our purses now. Therefore, not to hold you longer with many words, . . . remember what I have said in proving my proposition and take my conclusion in a word or two. . . .

Our forefathers, not looking out in time, lost the prime and fairest proffer of the greatest wealth in the world, and we tax their omission for it. Yet now it falls out that we their children are tried in the like, there being yet an excellent portion left, and by Divine providence offered to our choice, which (seeing we have arms to embrace) let it not be accounted hereafter as a prize in the hands of fools, that had no hearts to use it.

The honor of our nation is now very great by his Majesty's means, and we his subjects cannot enlarge and uphold it by gazing on, and talking what hath been done, but by doing that good, which may be commended hereafter. If we sit still and let slip occasions, we shall gather rust, and do unfeather our own wings. . . .

Let not such a prize of hopeful events, so lately purchased by the hazard of our valiant men, in the deep seas of foreign dangers, now perish in the haven by our neglect. The lives of our friends already planted, and of those noble knights and gentlemen that intend to go shortly, must lie at our mercy to be relieved and supplied by us, or to be made a prey unto others (though we fear not the subjects of any prince in amity, that they will offer wrong unto us). And howsoever we hear tales and rumors of this and that, yet be not dismayed; for I tell you, if we find that any miscreants have wronged, or go about to hurt our few hundreds there, we shall be ready to right it again with many thousands. . . .

And consider well that great work of freeing the poor Indians from the devourer, a compassion that every good man (but passing by) would show unto a beast. Their children, when they come to be saved, will bless the day when first their fathers saw your faces. . . .

1. *Nova Britannia: Offering Most Excellent fruits by Planting in Virginia, Exciting all such as be well affected to further the same* (London, 1609).

2. Hume, Ivor Noel, *The Virginia Adventure: Roanoke to James Towne, An Archaeological and Historical Odyssey* (Charlottesville: University Press of Virginia, 1994), 7. In 1494, Pope Alexander VI signed the Treaty of Tordesillas, which divided the entire New World between Spain and Portugal.

3. The pamphleteer is here referring to the voyages of John Cabot.

4. The author of *Book of English Voyages, by sundry English Captains and Gentlemen in that Voyage* was Richard Hakluyt; by 1608, Raleigh was a prisoner in the Tower of London.

5. Miller, Lee, *Roanoke: Solving the Mystery of the Lost Colony* (New York: Arcade Publishing, 2001), 5-18. In March 1590, John White found passage on a privateering ship called the *Hopewell* whose captain agreed to return him to Roanoke Island. The *Hopewell* and two other ships plundered Spanish ships in the Caribbean until August; one of the other English privateers was captained by Christopher Newport, who lost his arm during one of these engagements. The *Hopewell* did not reach Roanoke Island until hurricane season, and was only able to spend 11 days searching for the Lost Colonists before a storm blew the ship east towards the Azores. The last best chance to find the Lost Colony was gone.

A Spy in the Palace

From
Letter from Pedro de Zuniga to the King of Spain, 1609

"One of the more sinister figures lurking in the background of English-American history in the early 17th century" is how Ivor Noel Hume describes Pedro de Zuniga, Spain's ambassador in London during Jamestown's formative years.[2] With an extensive network of spies and informants, Zuniga kept King Philip III of Spain well supplied with plans, reports, maps, and even drawings of fortifications, all of which were stored safely in Spain's Royal Archives and now provide historians with a wealth of information about early English colonization.

This letter was found in the Royal Archive by

J. L. M. Curry, the United States minister to Spain during the 1890s. In it, Zuniga very accurately describes the Virginia Company's plan to send a large supply of new colonists under Sir Thomas Gates, followed by an even larger supply under Sir Thomas West, Lord de la Warr. Zuniga has also obtained a copy of Nova Britannia, which he sends to Philip with the letter. The nationalistic rhetoric of that pamphlet encourages Zuniga's fears of Jamestown as a base for a new generation of sea dogs to follow in the wakes of Raleigh and Sir Francis Drake, plundering the treasure galleons of the Spanish Main.

The Baron de Arundel to whom Zuniga refers had sponsored a failed attempt to land a Catholic colony in 1605; Philip would reject the plot that Arundel proposes, and cautioned Zuniga that the baron might be a double agent.[3] Though neither the Arundel plot, nor the ambassador's urgings to attack and uproot the young colony, came to pass, reading this letter—and knowing there were many more like it—makes the English obsessions with the Spanish and with hidden Catholics seem a little less paranoid. The first Jamestown colonists left England little more than a year after the discovery of the Gunpowder Plot, an attempt by English Catholics to blow up the Houses of Parliament (still celebrated annually in England as Guy Fawkes' Day, for the "trigger man" who was caught, tortured, and executed.) Each colonist, from the members of the council to the meanest laborer, was required to take an oath of supremacy, in which they swore their ultimate allegiance to James I rather than the Pope. For most of Jamestown's history, the primary fear for investors and adventurers was not

of Powhatan or famine or disease, but of a single massive
Spanish attack that would wipe the Jamestown peninsula
clean.

Highgate, March 5, 1609

Sire –

On December 12 I wrote to your Majesty how two vessels
left here for Virginia, and afterwards I heard that they carried
up to 150 men most of whom were men of distinction. And
likewise I wrote to your Majesty on January 17 how they would
make still greater efforts, and spoke of sending the Baron de
Arundel with a number of people, who has told me that they
have excluded him, because in order to go, he asked this King
[James I of England] for a patent and for money, and likewise
he tells me he had asked that liberty of conscience should be
given in that country. This is what he asserts; but the truth is
that they have failed to send him out because he is suspected of
being a Catholic. He is dissatisfied and has told me that if your
Majesty would do him the favor to reward him for the service
in Flanders, he would be of particular usefulness in this affair.
It seems to me he is all jealousy, that they have made the Baron
de la Warr general and governor of Virginia, who is a kinsman
of Don Antonio Shirley. They assure me, he has said that your
Majesty pays no attention, so far, to the people who go there
and this has made them so reckless that they no longer send
there little by little as heretofore, but they command that Captain
Gates go there, who is a very special soldier and has seen service
among the rebels [in the Netherlands]. He takes four to five

hundred men and 100 women, and all who go have first to take the oath of supremacy of the King. He will sail within a month or a month-and-a-half, and as soon as the news of his arrival is received here the Baron de la Warr is to sail with 600 or 700 men, and a large part of them principal men, and a few women, and when he gets there, the[n] Gates will return here to take more men. They have offered him, that all the pirates who are outside of this kingdom will be pardoned by the king, if they will take refuge there, and the thing is so perfect—according to what they say—for making use of these pirates, that your Majesty will not be able to get the silver from the Indies, unless a very large force should be kept there, and that they will make your Majesty's vassals lose their trade, since this is the design with which they go.

The Baron de Arundel offers to leave here, whenever your Majesty may command, under the pretext of a voyage of discovery, and that in the Canaries or in Puerto Rico he will take on board his ship the person whom your Majesty will send to him, as a man who is fleeing from Spain, and will carry him to Virginia and instruct him as to the mouth of the river, the posts which the English hold and the fortifications which they have, and that soon he will tell your Majesty by what means those people can be driven out without violence in arms. I am of the opinion that the business is very far advanced and that your Majesty ought not to apprehend much on account of these chances, since during the time of these goings and comings they will place there a large number of people, because they have too many of them and do not know what to do for them; and the time may come when this king will take a hand in this business openly, and your Majesty might find it very difficult to drive them out from there, and it might come to breaking all these treaties on this ground, which is largely asserted. Hence your Majesty will command that they should be destroyed with the utmost possible promptness, and when this news arrives here, although they may resent it, they will say that they ought not to have been there, because when I spoke with the king about their going to the Indies and to those countries, he said to me that he could not hold them otherwise than according to the treaty, if they gathered together there they were liable to be punished. I send your Majesty a 'placard,' which has been issued to all officials, showing what they give them for going, and there has been gotten together in 20 days a sum of money for this voyage which amazes one; among 14 counts and barons they have given 40,000 ducats, the merchants give much more, and there is no poor, little man, nor woman, who is not willing to subscribe something for this enterprise. . . . Three counties have pledged themselves that they will give a good sum of money, and they are negotiating with the prince [of Wales, Henry] that he shall make himself 'Protector of Virginia,' and in this manner they will go deeper and deeper into the business, if your Majesty does not order them to be stopped very promptly. They have printed a book, which I also send your Majesty, in which they call that country New Britain, and in which they publish that for the increase of their religion and that it may extend over the whole world, it is right that all should support this colony with their person and their property. It would be a service rendered to God, that your Majesty should cut short a swindle and a robbery like this, and one which is so important to your Majesty's royal service. If they go on far with this they must needs get proud of it and disregard what they owe here, and if your Majesty chastises them, he puts a bridle upon them and thus will make them see to it before they undertake anything against the King's service. I confess to your Majesty that I write this with indignation, because I see the people are mad about this affair and shameless. I have also seen a letter written by a gentleman who is over there in Virginia, to another friend of his, who is known to me, and has shown it to me. He says that from Captain Newport, who is the bearer of it, he will learn in detail how matters are there, and that all he can say is that there has been found a moderate mine of silver and that the best part of England cannot be compared with that country. He says furthermore that they have deceived the King of that part of the country by means of an English boy, whom they have given him saying that he is a son of this king, and he treats him very handsomely; he has sent a present to this king. [See the next entry for more about this "English boy."]

I understand that as soon as they are well fortified they will kill that king and the savages, so as to obtain possession of everything. . . . I have thought it my duty to report this to your Majesty by this courier, because your Majesty ought very promptly to give orders to make an end of this.

NOTES

1. Brown, Alexander, *Genesis of the United States* (Cambridge: The Riverside Press, 1890), 243-47.
2. Hume, Ivor Noel, *The Virginia Adventure: Roanoke to James Towne, An Archaeological and Historical Odyssey* (Charlottesville: University Press of Virginia, 1994), 115.
3. Ibid., 238.

"He Sold Me to Him for a Town"

From
Henry Spelman's *Relation of Virginia*

> *Henry Spelman was only about fourteen years old*
> *when he arrived in Virginia as one of the 400 colonists*
> *in the supply of 1609, the one led by Somers and Gates*
> *and scattered by tempest en route. Less than two weeks*
> *after his landing at Jamestown, Spelman was taken by*
> *Smith to the falls of the James, where Smith traded the*
> *boy to Parahunt, the son of Powhatan who ruled the*
> *town called Powhatan, near the present site of Richmond.*
> *In exchange for the boy, Smith received a plot of land on*
> *which he ordered Captain Francis West to build a fort*
> *and town. Such an exchange was not unprecedented; the*
> *year before, Newport had given his "son"—a thirteen-*
> *year-old laborer named Thomas Savage—to Powhatan*

himself, in exchange for the chief's "son"—a young but trusted servant named Namontack. All three boys were expected to learn the opposite culture and language as fully as they could, and report back at a later date.[2]

Though Spelman had little education, he was clearly intelligent: he returned to Jamestown not long after his exchange, but apparently sized up the situation better than most of his elders had and returned to the Indians before the Starving Time set in. At first Spelman stayed with Powhatan at Oropikes, where he was a witness to the death by torture of John Ratcliffe.[3] (More about Ratcliffe's death is described in the excerpt on page 157 by George Percy.) Soon after, Spelman managed to leave Powhatan in the company of the king of Patawomeke, with whom he lived until the end of 1610, when he returned to Jamestown with Captain Samuel Argall. He returned to England twice, but always came back, serving as the colony's principal interpreter and rising to the rank of captain. Thirteen years after he was sold to Parahunt, Captain Spelman was killed leading a trading expedition to his old friend, the king of Patawomeke.

Despite the hindrance of his youth, which he admits kept him from seeing or recognizing all that he might have, Spelman's Relation of Virginia is one of the richest sources available about the Powhatans and Patawomekes. In the first half, Spelman describes how he came to live with the Patawomekes and his adventures while there; in the second half, he describes their customs, beliefs, practices.

Being in displeasure of my friends, and desirous to see other countries, after three months' sail we come with prosperous winds in sight of Virginia, where a storm suddenly arising severed our fleet ... every ship from other, putting us all in great danger for *vij* or *viij* days together. But ye storm then ceasing, our ship called ye *Unity* came ye next morning safely to an anchor at Cape Henry, ye day of October 1609, where we found the other of our fleet, and about a sennight [a week] after three more came thether also. The residue, amongst which was Sir Thomas Gates and Sir George Somers, Knights, were not heard of many months after our arrival.

From Cape Henry we sailed up ye River Powhatan [James River] and within four or five days arrived at Jamestown, where we were joyfully welcomed by our countrymen, being at that time about 80 persons under the government of Captain Smith, the president. Having here unladed our goods and bestowed some sennight or fortnight in viewing of the country, I was carried by Captain Smith our president to ye falls, to ye little Powhatan, where unknown to me he sold me to him for a town called Powhatan, and, leaving me with him ye little Powhatan, he made known to Captain West how he had bought a town for them to dwell in . . . desiring that Captain West would come and settle himself there, but Captain West, having bestowed cost to begin a town in another place, misliked it; and unkindness thereupon arising between them, Captain Smith at that time replied little, but afterward conspired with the Powhatan to kill Captain West, which plot took but small effect, for in ye meantime Captain Smith was apprehended, and sent aboard for England, myself having been now about *vij* or *viij* days with the little Powhatan, who though he made very much of me, giving me such things as he had to win me to live with him, yet I desired to see our English, and therefore made signs unto him to give me leave to go to our ship to fetch such things as I left behind me, which he agreed unto, and setting himself down, he clapped his hand on the ground in token he would stay there till I returned.[4] But I staying somewhat too long, at my coming to ye place where I left him I found him departed, whereupon I went back to our ship, being still in ye falls, and sailed with them to Jamestown, where not being long there . . . one Thomas Savage with four or five Indians came from the great Powhatan with venison to Captain Percy, who now was president. After the delivery thereof, and that he must return, he was loath to go without some of his countrymen went with him, whereupon I was appointed to go, which I the more willingly did, by reason that vitals were scarce with us, carrying with me some copper and a hatchet which I had gotten. Coming to the Great Powhatan, I presented to him such things as I had, which he took, using me very kindly, setting this Savage and me at his own table. . . . And after I had been with him about three weeks, he sent me back to our English, bidding me tell them that if they would bring their ship, and some copper, he would freight her back with corn, which I having reported to our English and returning their answer to ye King, he before their coming laid plots to take them, which in some sort he affected, for *xxvj* or *vij* they killed which came towards land in their long boat, and shot many arrows into ye ship, which our men, perceiving and fearing the worst, weighed anchor and returned. Now while this business was in action, ye Powhatan sends me and one Samuell, a Dutchman, to a town about *xvj* miles off, called Yaughtawnoone, willing us there to stay for him. At his coming thether we understood how all things had passed by Thomas Savage, as before is related, the King in show made still much of us, yet his mind was much declined from us, which made us fear the worst, and having now been with him about 24 or 25 weeks, it happened that the King of Patawomeke came to visit the great Powhatan, where being a while with him, he showed such kindness to Savage, Samuell, and myself, as we determined to go away with him. When the day of his departure was come, we did as we agreed, and having gone a mile or two on the way, Savage feigned some excuse of stay, and, unknown to us, went back to the Powhatan and acquainted him with our departing with ye Patawomeke. The Powhatan presently sends after us commanding our return, which we refusing, went still on our way. And those that were sent, went still on with us, till one of them, finding opportunity, on a sudden struck Samuell with an axe and killed him, which I seeing, ran away from among the company, they after me, the King and his men after them, who, overtaking them, held them, till I shifted for myself and got to the Patawomeke's country. With this King Patawomeke I lived a year and more at a town of his called Pasptanzie, until such time as a worthy gentleman named Captain Argall arrived at a town called Nacottawtanke, but by our English called Camocacocke, where he understood that there was an English boy named Harry. He, desiring to hear further of me, came up the river, which the King of Patawomeke hearing, sent me to him, and I, going back again, brought the king to ye ship, where Captain Argall gave the King some copper for me, which he received. Thus was I set at liberty and brought into England. . . .

Of their service to their gods

To give some satisfaction to my friends, and contentment unto others, which wish well to this voyage, and are desirous to hear ye fashions of that country, I have set down, as well as I can, what I observed in ye time I was among them. And therefore first concerning their gods, you must understand that for ye most part they worship ye devil, which ye conjurers who are their priests can make appear unto them at their pleasure, yet never ye less in every country they have a several image whom they call their god. As with the great Powhatan, he hath an image called Cakeres, which most commonly standeth at Yaughtawnoone in one of ye King's houses, or at Oropikes in a house for that purpose, and with him are set all the King's goods and presents that are sent him, as ye corn. But ye beads or crown or bed which ye King of England sent him are in ye god's house at Oropikes, and in their houses are all ye King's ancestors and kindred commonly buried.

In ye Patawomeke's country they have another god whom they call Quioquascacke, and unto their images they offer beads and copper if at any time they want rain or have too much, and though they observe no day to worship their god but upon necessity, yet once in the year, their priests which are their conjurers, with ye men, women, and children, do go into the woods, where their priests make a great circle of fire, in ye which, after many observances in their conjurations, they make offer of two or three children to be given to their god if he will appear unto them and show his mind whom he desire. Upon which offering, they hear a "Caukewis Manato Taukinge souke Quia uasack" noise out of ye circle nominating such as he will have, whom presently they take, binding them hand and foot, and cast them into ye circle of the fire, for be it the King's son he must be given if once named by their god. After ye bodies which are offered are consumed in the fire and their ceremonies performed, the men depart merrily, the women weeping. . . .

Of their towns & buildings

Places of habitation they have but few, for ye greatest town have not above 20 or 30 houses in it. Their buildings are made like an oven with a little hole to come in at, but more spacious within, having a hole in the midst of ye house for smoke to go out at. The King's houses are both broader and longer than ye rest, having many dark windings and turnings before any come where the King is. But in that time when they go a-hunting ye women goes to a place appointed before, to build houses for their husbands to lie in at night, carrying mats with them to cover their houses withal, and as the men goes further a-hunting the women follows to make houses, always carrying their mats with them.

Their manner of their hunting is this: they meet some two or three hundred together, and having their bows and arrows, and everyone with a firestick in their hand, they beset a great thicket round about, which done, everyone set fire on the rank grass, which ye deer seeing, fleeth from ye fire, and the men coming in by a little and little, encloseth their game in a narrow room, so as with their bows and arrows they kill them at their pleasure, taking their skins, which is the greatest thing they desire, and some flesh for their provision.

Their manner of marrying

The custom of ye country is to have many wives and to buy them, so that he which have most copper and beads may have most wives, for if he taketh liking of any woman he makes love to her, and seeketh to her father or kinsfolk to set what price he must pay for her, which being once agreed on the kindred meet and make good cheer, and when the sum agreed on be paid she shall be delivered to him for his wife. The ceremony is thus: the parents brings their daughter between them (if her parents be dead then some of her kinsfolk, or whom it pleaseth ye king to appoint, for ye man goes not unto any place to be married, but ye woman is brought to him where he dwelleth). At her coming to him, her father or chief friends joins the hands together and then ye father or chief friend of ye man bringeth a long string of beads and measuring his arm's length thereof doth break it over ye hands of those that are to be married while their hands be joined together, and gives it unto ye woman's father or him that brings her. And so with much mirth and feasting they go together. When ye King of ye country will have any wives he acquaints his chief men with his purpose, who sends into all parts of ye country for ye fairest and comliest maids out of which ye King taketh his choice, giving to their parents what he pleaseth. If any of ye King's wives have once a child by him, he keeps her no longer but puts her from him, giving her sufficient copper and beads to maintain her and the child while it is young, and then it is taken from her and maintained by ye King, it now being lawful for her being thus put away to marry with any other. . . .

This Pasptanse was brother to Patawomeke. It was my happ to be left at one of ye Pasptanse's houses when he went to visit another King, and two of his wives were there also. After the King's departure, one of them would go visit her father . . . and seeing me, willed me to go with her and to take her child and carry him thether in my arms, being a day's journey from ye place where we dwelt. I refusing, she struck me three or four blows, but I being loath to bear too much got to her and pulled her down, giving her some blows again, which ye other of ye King's wives perceiving, they both fell on me, beating me so as I thought they had lamed me. Afterward when ye King came home, in their presence I acquainted him how they had used me. The King without further delay took up a couwascohocan, which is a kind of paring iron, and struck at one of them with such violence, as he felled her to the ground in manner dead. I seeing that, fled to a neighbor's house, for fear of ye King's displeasure. But his wife coming again to herself, somewhat appeased his anger, so as understanding where I was by his brother, he sent me his young child to still, for none could quiet him so well as myself, and about midnight he sent for him again. The next day the King was early up, and came to the house where I was. Loath I was to see him, yet . . . instead of his anger, I found him kind to me, asking me how I did, and whether I was afraid of him last night, because I ran away from him, and hid myself. I, being by his speeches somewhat bolder, asked him for his Queen. He answered all was well, and that I should go home with him, telling me he loved me, and none should hurt me. I, though loath, went with him, where at my coming ye Queen looked but discontentedly on me. But hoping on the King's promise, I cared ye less for others' frowns, knowing well that ye King made ye more of me in hope I should help him to some copper, if at any time our English came into those parts, which I often had promised him to do, and which was by Captain Argall bountifully performed. . . .

Their manner of visiting the sick, with ye fashion of their burial if they die

When any be sick among them, their priests comes unto the party, whom he layeth on the ground upon a mat. And having a bowl of water set between him and the sick party, and a rattle by it, the priest kneeling by the sick man's side dips his hand into the bowl, which taking up full of water, he sups into his mouth, spouting it out again, upon his own arms, and breast. Then takes he the rattle, and with one hand takes that, and with the other he beats his breast, making a great noise, which having done he easily riseth (as loath to wake the sick body) first with one leg, then with the other. And being now got up, he leisurely goeth about ye sick man shaking his rattle very softly over all his body, and with his hand he stroketh ye grieved parts of the sick. Then doth he besprinkle him with water mumbling certain words over him, and so for that time leave him. But if he be wounded after this ceremony's done unto him he with a little flint stone gasheth the wound making it to run and bleed, which he, setting his mouth unto it, sucks out, and then applies a certain root beaten to powder unto ye sore.

If he dies his burial is thus: there is a scaffold built about three or four yards high from the ground, and the dead body wrapped in a mat is brought to the place, where, when he is laid thereon, the kinsfolk falls a-weeping and make great sorrow, and instead of a dole for him, (the poorer people being got together) some of his kinsfolk flings beads among them making them to scramble for them, so that many times divers do break their arms and legs being pressed by the company. This finished they go to ye party's house where they have meat given them, which being eaten all ye rest of the day they spend in singing and dancing, using then as much mirth as before sorrow. Moreover if any of ye kindred's bodies which have been laid on ye scaffold should be consumed as nothing is left but bones they take those bones from ye scaffold, and putting them into a new mat, hangs them in their houses, where they continue while their house falleth and then they are buried in the ruins of ye house. What goods the party leaveth is divided among his wives and children. But his house he giveth to the wife he liketh best for life; after her death, unto what child he most loveth.

The justice and government

Concerning their laws, my years and understanding made me the less to look after because I thought that infidels were lawless. Yet when I saw some put to death I asked the cause of their offence, for in the time that I was with ye Patawomeke I saw five executed: four for murder of a child—ye mother, and two other that did the fact with her, and a fourth for concealing it as he passed by, being bribed to hold his peace—and one for robbing a traveler of copper and beads, for to steal their neighbor's corn or copper is death, or to lie one with another's wife is death if he be taken in the manner.

The manner of execution

Those that be convicted of capital offences are brought into a plain place before ye King's house . . . where one or two appointed by the King did bind them hand and foot, which being done a great fire was made. Then came the officer to those that should die, and with a shell cut off their long lock, which they wear on the left side of their head, and hangeth that on a bow before the King's house. Then those for murder were beaten with staves till their bones were broken, and being alive were flung into the fire. The other for robbing was knocked on ye head, and being dead his body was burnt.

The manner of setting their corn with ye gathering and dressing

They take most commonly a place about their houses to set their corn, which if there be much wood, in that place they cut down the great trees some half a yard above the ground, and ye smaller they burn at the root, pulling a good part of bark from them to make them die, and in this place they dig many holes, which before the English brought them scavels and spades, they used to make with a crooked piece of wood, being scraped on both sides in fashion of a gardener's paring iron. They put into these holes ordinarily four or five kernels of their wheat and two beans like French beans, which when the wheat do grow up, having a straw as big as a cane reed, the beans run up thereon like our hops on poles. The ear of ye wheat is of great bigness in length and compass, and yet for all the greatness of it every stalk hath most commonly some four or five ears on it. Their corn is set and gathered about the time we use, but their manner of their gathering is as we do our apples: first in hand baskets, emptying them as they are filled into other bigger baskets, whereof some are made of the barks of trees, some of hemp which naturally groweth there, and some of the straw whereon ye wheat groweth. Now after ye gathering, they lay it upon mats a good thickness in the sun to dry, and every night they make a great pile of it, covering it over with mats to defend it from the dew, and when it is sufficiently weathered they pile it up in their houses, daily as occasion serveth wringing the ears in pieces between their hands, and so rubbing out their corn do put it to a great basket which taketh up the best part of some of their houses, and all this is chiefly the women's work for the men do only hunt to get skins in winter and do ... dress them in summer.

But, though now out of order, yet let me not altogether forget the setting of ye King's corn, for which a day is appointed wherein great part of ye country people meet, who with such diligence worketh as for the most part all ye King's corn is set on a day. After which setting the King takes the crown which ye King of England sent him, being brought him by two men, and sets it on his head, which done, the people goeth about the corn in manner backwards for they going before, and the king following. Their faces are always toward the King, expecting when he should fling some beads among them which his custom is at that time to do, making those which had wrought to scramble for them. But to some he favors he bids those that carry his beads to call such-and-such unto him, unto whom he giveth beads into their hand, and this is the greatest courtesy he doth his people. When his corn is ripe the country people comes to him again and gathers dries and rubs out all his corn for him, which is laid in houses appointed for that purpose.

The setting at meat

They sit on mats round about ye house; ye men by themselves and ye women by theirselves. Ye women bring to everyone a dish of meat, for the better sort never eats together in one dish. When he hath eaten what he will, or that which was given him, for he looks for no second course, he sets down his dish by him and mumbleth certain words to himself in manner of giving thanks. If any left ye women gather it up and either keeps it till ye next meal, or gives it to ye poorer sort, if any be there.

The differences among them

The King is not known by any difference from other of ye chief sort in ye country, but only when he comes to any of their houses, they present him with copper beads or victual, and show much reverence to him.

The priests are shaven on ye right side of their head close to the skull, only a little lock left at ye ear, and some of these have beards. But ye common people have no beards at all, for they pull away their hairs as fast as it grows. And they also cut ye hairs on ye right side of their head that it might not hinder them by flapping about their bowstring when they draw it to shoot. But on ye other side they let it grow and have a long lock hanging down their shoulder.

The armor and weapon with discipline in war

As for armor or discipline in war they have not any. The weapons they use for offense are bows and arrows, with a weapon like a hammer, and then tomahawks for defense, which are shields made of the bark of a tree and hanged on their left shoulder to cover that side as they stand forth to shoot.

They never fight in open fields but always either among reeds or behind trees, taking their opportunity to shoot at their enemies, and till they can nock another arrow they make the trees their defense.

In ye time that I was there I saw a battle fought between the Patawomeke and the Masomeck. Their place where they fought was a marsh ground full of reed. Being in the country of the Patawomeke the people of Masomeck were brought thether in canoes, which is a kind of boat they have made in the form of a hog's trough, but somewhat more hollowed in. On both sides they scatter themselves some little distant one from the other, then take they their bows and arrows and, having made ready to shoot, they softly steal toward their enemies, sometime squatting down and prying if they can spy any to shoot at. . . . If at any time he so hurteth that he can not flee, they make haste to him to knock him on the head, and they that kill most of their enemies are held the chiefest men among them. Drums and trumpets they have none, but when they will gather themselves together they have a kind of howling or howbabub so differing in sound one from the other as both part may very easily be distinguished. There was no greater slaughter of neither side, but ye Masomecks having shot away most of the arrows and wanting victual were glad to retire.

The pastimes

When they meet at feasts or otherwise they use sports much like to our here in England, as their dancing, which is like our Derbyshire Hornpipe: a man first and then a woman, and so through them all, hanging all in a round. There is one which stand in the midst with a pipe and a rattle, with which when he begins to make a noise all the rest gigetts about . . . stamping on ye ground.

They use beside football play, which women and young boys do much play at, the men, never. They make their goals as ours, only they never fight nor pull one another down.

The men play with a little ball, letting it fall out of their hand and striketh it with the top of his foot, and he that can strike the ball furthest wins that they play for.

NOTES

1. Spelman, Henry, *Relation of Virginia* (London: Printed for Jas. F. Hunnewell at the Chiswick Press, 1872).

2. Hume, Ivor Noel, *The Virginia Adventure: Roanoke to James Towne, An Archaeological and Historical Odyssey* (Charlottesville: University Press of Virginia, 1994), 194.

3. Ibid., 258.

4. "Little Powhatan" is Parahunt, Powhatan's son, who ruled the town of Powhatan at the falls of the James River, introduced in George Percy's *Discourse of the Plantation of the Southern Colony in Virginia by the English.*

"That Sharp Prick of Hunger"

From

A True Relation of the Proceedings and Occurrences of Moment which have happened in Virginia from the Time Sir Thomas Gates was shipwrecked upon the Bermudas, anno 1609, until my departure out of the Country which was in anno Domini 1612 by George Percy[1]

Jamestown's first two years were an unequivocal misery of disease, want, and fear. What special horror, then, must the colonists have found in the fall, winter, and spring of 1609-1610, that those particular months would come to be known as the Starving Time?

The numbers answer part of the question: out of

roughly 600 colonists (now including women and children) living in Tidewater Virginia in the summer of 1609, only about 60 were still alive to greet their relief in May 1610—a 90 percent mortality rate.[2] But numbers do not convey the unrelenting pain of hunger, the impotency of debilitating illness, the claustrophobic fear of knowing an implacable enemy waits just beyond your gates. To get a sense of the Starving Time, we must turn to the accounts written by the survivors, and the best of those is A True Relation . . . by George Percy.

The company passed Percy over for a seat on the original council, which may have spared Percy's standing in the colony by removing him from the bitter dissensions of the first year. By the spring of 1609 the company had decided to abolish the council in Virginia altogether, and replace it with a single, all-powerful governor. The first of these governor-generals was to be Sir Thomas West, Lord de la Warr. Since West was not able to leave England immediately, the company sent a nine-ship fleet, commanded by the redoubtable Captain Christopher Newport, to carry close to 600 new colonists and Sir Thomas Gates, an original patentee of the company, to rule as lieutenant governor until West's arrival.

This fleet was scattered, though, by a violent storm near the end of their Atlantic crossing, and the flagship— the Sea Venture, which carried Gates, Newport, and the other senior leaders—wrecked on the shore of Bermuda (see "Tempest and Redemption," which follows on page 167). As the other ships straggled up the James River, Jamestown received an influx of about 400 inexperienced settlers, many of them the "undesirables" rounded up by the Lord Mayor of London, but no new leadership and precious few supplies. Even worse, among the 400 who made it to Jamestown were the colony's original conspirators, Gabriel Archer, John Martin, and John Ratcliffe. John Smith, by now the president of the colony, refused to relinquish command, especially to these three, in the absence of the company's written orders and the new commander himself, Gates. Smith divided the fighting men of the colony into three forces: one to stay with him at Jamestown, one under Captain Francis West to establish a fort near the falls of the James (see "He Sold Me to Him for a Town," on page 135), and one under the command of Percy and John Martin to establish an outpost further down the James, in the territory of the Nansemond Indians.

While trying to put these plans into practice, Smith was badly injured when a pouch of gunpowder hanging from his belt caught fire—accidentally or not is still unknown. Incapacitated, he left for England in one of the departing ships, never to return to Virginia. Percy was persuaded to take over the presidency of the colony, and would continue in command as the summer passed, and Jamestown sank slowly into the Starving Time.

Blame for the Starving Time has been laid at many feet: lazy Jamestown gentlemen, gold-hungry Jamestown settlers, the absence of Smith's leadership, Mother Nature. A recent episode of the PBS series Secrets of the Dead offered two new possibilities: arsenic poisoning, perhaps by a Spanish agent (less outlandish in light of Zuniga's letter in "A Spy in the Palace" on pages 129–32), or a sudden outbreak of the Black Plague. Recent tests have *concluded that a drought struck lower Virginia during these years, which would make the Indians less likely to trade their corn and also would increase the chances of salt poisoning from the already-brackish waters of the James River.[3] Percy suggests that the colony was simply overpopulated and undersupplied.*

A dozen years after he had left Virginia, Percy felt his honor impugned by the publication of John Smith's A General History of Virginia, *which questioned Percy's leadership before and during the Starving Time. In response, Percy wrote* A True Relation of the Proceedings and Occurrences of Moment which have happened in Virginia. . . . *Addressed to his brother Henry, the ninth Earl of Northumberland,* A True Relation *was forgotten until 1884, when historian Edward D. Neill discovered that the manuscript was in the library of a Lord Leconfield in Sussex. Twenty years later, Lyon G. Tyler, a prominent Virginia historian and one-time president of the College of William & Mary, got the assistance of the United States ambassador to Great Britain in securing a copy of the manuscript for the Virginia State Library. In 1922 it was published in* Tyler's Quarterly Historical and Genealogical Magazine, *from which this excerpt is taken.*

To the right honorable the Lord Percy:

My Lord—

This relation I have here sent your Lordship is for two respects. The one, to show how much I honor you and desire to do you service. The other, in regard that many untruths concerning these proceedings have been formerly published, wherein the author [Smith] hath not spared to appropriate many desserts to himself which he never performed, and stuffed his relations with so many falsities and malicious detractions, not only of this point and time which I have selected to treat of, but of former occurrences also, so that I could not contain myself, but express the truth unto your Lordship concerning these affairs. And all which I aim at is to manifest myself in all my actions, both now and always to be,

Your Lordship's humble and faithful servant,

G. P.

If we truly consider the diversity of miseries, mutinies, and famishments, which have attended upon discoveries and plantations in these our modern times, we shall not find our plantation in Virginia to have suffered alone. . . .

Many other woes and miseries have happened unto our colony in Virginia both before and since that time, which now I do intend to treat of, having selected this point from the rest for two respects: first, in regard I was most frequent and acquainted with these proceedings, being most point of the time president and governor; next, in respect the least point hereof hath not been formerly published. In the year of our Lord 1609, Sir Thomas Gates and Sir George Somers, accompanied with divers gentlemen, soldiers, and seamen in nine good ships, did begin their voyage for Virginia, the two knights being in the *Admiral*, whereof Christopher Newport was Captain. And having sailed with prosperous winds many leagues, at length did fall upon the Bermudas, where, meeting with a violent storm, the *Admiral* wherein the two knights were embarked suffered wrack; nevertheless, hoisting out their boat, safely landed the two knights and the rest of that company upon the Bermudas, of whom I will forbear to treat of further until their arrival in Virginia.

The other eight ships shortly after arrived in Virginia, where the passengers being no sooner well landed but presently a dissension did grow between them and Captain Smith, then president, but after some debate all was quieted and pacified. Yet Captain Smith, fearing the worst, and that the seamen and that faction might grow too strong and be a means to depose him of his government, so juggled with them by the way of feastings, expense of much powder, and other unnecessary triumphs, that much was spent to no other purpose but to insinuate with his reconciled enemies and for his own vain glory, for the which, we all after suffered. And that which was intolerable, did give leave unto the seamen to carry away what victuals and other necessaries they would. . . .

Not long after, Captain Smith sent Captain Martin and myself with threescore people to go for Nansemond, Captain Martin's lieutenant leading most of the men overland, and we two with the rest followed them by water. . . . Being arrived we inquired of the Indians of our men, but they, according to their subtleties, would not acquaint us therewith. . . . I requested Captain Martin that I might go ashore to discover the truth, to the which he would not condescend. Nevertheless, the night being stormy and wet, I went on land with my company, where I found our men by good fires in safety, whereof I advertised Captain Martin the next morning, who presently with his company did come ashore unto us, where after some consultation held we sent two messengers to the king of Nansemond to barter with him for an island right opposite against the main we were upon for copper, hatchets, and other commodities. But our messengers staying longer than we expected, we feared that which after happened. So Captain Martin did appoint (me) with half of our men to take the island perforce. . . . Being upon the way we espied a canoe wherein we were persuaded our messengers to be, but they, perceiving us, returned back from whence they came, and we never set eye upon our messengers after, but understood from the Indians themselves that they were sacrificed, and that their brains were cut and scraped out of their heads with mussell shells. Being landed and acquainted with their treachery, we beat the savages out of the island, burned their houses, ransacked their temples, took down the corpses of their dead kings from off their tombs, and carried away their pearls, copper, and bracelets, wherewith they do decor their kings' funerals.

In the meantime, savages upon the main did fall into dissension with Captain Martin, who seized the king's son and one other Indian and brought them bound unto the island where I was. . . . A ship boy, taking up a pistol, accidentally, not meaning any harm . . . suddenly fired and shot the savage prisoner into the breast. And thereupon, what with his passion and fear, he broke the cords asunder where with he was tied and did swim over unto the main with his wound bleeding. And there being great store of maize upon the main I counseled Captain Martin to take possession thereof, the which he refused, pretending that he would not put his men into hazard and danger. So, having seen Captain Martin well settled, I returned with Captain Nelson to Jamestown again according to appointment.

Shortly after, Captain Smith sent Captain Francis West with

one hundred and forty men up to the falls with six months' victuals to inhabit there. Where, being reasonable well settled, divers of his men straggled from their fort, some of them coming home wounded, others never returned to bring any tidings but were cut off and slain by the savages. So that in small process of time, Captain Smith did take his journey up to the falls to understand how things were there ordered, when presently after his coming thether, a great division did grow amongst them. Captain Smith, perceiving both his authority and person neglected, incensed and animated the savages against Captain West and his company, reporting unto them that our men had no more powder left them than would serve for one volley of shot. And so Captain Smith, returning to Jamestown, again found to have too much powder about him, the which being in his pocket where the spark of a match lighted, very shrewdly burned him. And coming in that case to Jamestown, Captains Ratcliffe, Archer, and Martin practiced against him and deposed him of his government, Smith being an ambitious, unworthy, and vainglorious fellow, attempting to take all men's authorities from them. . . . Although indeed, there was no other certain appointed government than Sir Thomas Gates had commission for, who was then in the Bermudas, only a yearly presidentship to govern by the advice of the Council. But Smith, aiming at a sovereign rule without the assistance of the Council, was justly deprived of all.

The place of government being void, the three busy instruments [Ratcliffe, Archer, and Martin] in the plantation offered the same unto me, the which at first I refused in regard of my sickness. But by their importunings, promising to undergo the chiefest offices and burthen of government for me until I were recovered, at length I accepted thereof, and then was Smith presently sent for England.

After I had been president some fourteen days I sent Captain Ratcliffe to Point Comfort for to build a fort there. The which I did for two respects: the one, for the plenty of the place for fishing, the other for the commodious discovery of any shipping which should come upon the coast. And for the honor of your Lordship's name and house, I named the same Algernon's Fort.[4]

Not long after, Captain Martin, whom I left at the island, did come to Jamestown pretending some occasions of business, but indeed his own safety moved him thereunto, fearing to be surprised by the Indians, who had made divers excursions against him, so that having left Lieutenant Sicklemore to command in his absence, amongst whose company shortly after did grow a dangerous mutiny, in so much that divers of his men—to the number of seventeen—did take away a boat from him perforce, and went therein to Kecoughtan, pretending they would trade therefore victuals. But they were served according to their deserts, for not any of them were heard of after, and in all likelihood were cut off and slain by the savages. And within few days after, Lieutenant Sicklemore and divers others were found also slain with their mouths stopped full of bread, being done as it seemeth in contempt and scorn that others might expect the like when they should come to seek for bread and relief amongst them. . . .

And all the rest of Sicklemore's company which were living returned to us to Jamestown to feed upon the poor store we had left us.

Also within a short time after, Captain West did come down to us from the falls, having lost eleven men and a boat at Arsateck besides those men he lost at the falls, so our number at

Jamestown increasing and our store decreasing, for in charity we could not deny them to participate with us. Whereupon I appointed Captain Tucker to calculate and cast up our store. The which, at a poor allowance of half a can of meal for a man a day, amounted unto three months provision, yet Captain Tucker by his industry and care caused the same to hold out four months. But having no expectation of relief to come in so short a time, I sent Captain Ratcliffe to Powhatan to procure victuals and corn by the way of commerce and trade, the which the subtle old fox at first made good semblance of, although his intent was otherwise only waiting a fitting time for their destruction, as after plainly appeared. The which was probably occasioned by Captain Ratcliffe's credulity, for having Powhatan's son and daughter aboard his pinnace, freely suffered them to depart again on shore, whom if he had detained might have been a sufficient pledge for his safety. And after not keeping a proper and fitting court of guard, but suffering his men by two and three and small numbers in a company to straggle into the savages' houses, when the sly old king espied a fitting time, cut them all off; only surprised Captain Ratcliffe alive, who he caused to be bound unto a tree naked with a fire before, and by women his flesh was scraped from his bones with mussell shells, and before his face, thrown into the fire. And so, for want of circumspection, miserably perished.

In the meantime Captain William Phettiplace remained in the pinnace with some few men, and was divers times assaulted by the Indians, but after divers conflicts, with the loss of some of his men, hardly escaped, and at length arrived at Jamestown, only with sixteen men, the remainder of fifty Captain Ratcliffe hath charge of at his going forth. And so he related unto us the tragedy of Captain Ratcliffe, not bringing any relief with them either for themselves or us.

Upon which defeat I sent Captain James Davies to Algernon's Fort to command there in Captain Ratcliffe's place. And Captain West I sent to Patawomeke with about thirty-six men to trade for maize and grain, where he in short time loaded his pinnace sufficiently, yet used some harsh and cruel dealing by cutting of two of the savages' heads and other extremities. And coming by Algernon's Fort, Captain Davies did call unto them, acquainting them with our great wants, exhorting them to make all the speed they could to relieve us, upon which report Captain West, by the persuasion or rather by the enforcement of his company, hoisted up sails and shaped their course directly for England, and left us in that extreme misery and want.

Now all of us at Jamestown beginning to feel that sharp prick of hunger, which no man truly describe but he which hath tasted the bitterness thereof. A world of miseries ensued, as the sequel will express unto you, in so much that some to satisfy their hunger have robbed the store, for the which I caused them to be executed. Then, having fed upon horses and other beasts as long as they lasted, we were glad to make shift with vermin, as dogs, cats, rats, and mice. All was fish that came to net to satisfy cruel hunger, as to eat boots, shoes, or any other leather some could come by. And those being spent and devoured, some were enforced to search the woods and to feed upon serpents and snakes, and to dig the earth for wild and unknown roots, where many of our men were cut off and slain by the savages. And now, famine beginning to look ghastly and pale in every face . . . nothing was spared to maintain life and to do those things which seem incredible, as to dig up dead corpses out of graves and to eat them, and some have licked up the blood which hath fallen from their weak fellows. And amongst the rest, this was most lamentable: that one of our colony murdered his wife, ripped the child out of her womb, and threw it into the river, and after, chopped the mother in pieces and salted her for his food. The same not being discovered before he had eaten part thereof, for the which cruel and inhumane fact, I adjudged him to be executed, the acknowledgement of the deed being enforced from him by torture, having hung by the thumbs with weights at his feet a quarter of an hour before he would confess the same.

Upon these calamities, having one boat and a canoe left us, our boat did accidentally break loose and did drive four miles down the river before she was espied. Whereupon Captain Martin, appointing some to follow her, the which being neglected, and acquainting me therewith I stepped out of my house with my sword drawn; and what with my threats and their fears, happy was he could ship himself into the canoe first. And so our boat that night was again recovered, yet wanting more boats for fishing and other needful occasions, Captain Daniel Tucker by his great industry and pains builded a large boat with his own hands, the which was some help and a little relief unto us, and did keep us from killing one of another. To eat, many our men this starving time did run away unto the savages, whom we never heard of after.

By this time being reasonable well recovered of my sickness, I did undertake a journey unto Algernon's Fort, both to understand how things were there ordered, as also to have been revenged of the savages at Kecoughtan who had treacherously slain divers of our men. Our people I found in good case and well liking, having concealed their plenty from us above at Jamestown. Being so well stored that the crab fishes wherewith they had fed their hogs would have been a great relief unto us and saved many of our lives. But their intent was for to have kept some of the better sort alive, and with their two pinnaces to have returned for England, not regarding our miseries and wants at all. Wherewith I taxed Captain Davies, and told him that I had a full intent to bring half of our men from Jamestown to be there relieved, and after to return them back again and bring the rest to be sustained there also. And if all this would not serve to save our men's lives, I purposed to bring them all unto Algernon's Fort, telling Captain Davies that another town or fort might be erected and builded, but men's lives, once lost, could never be recovered.

Our miseries now being at the highest, and intending as I formerly related unto you to remove some of our men to Algernon's Fort, the very next tide we espied two pinnaces coming into the bay, not knowing as yet what they were, but keeping a court of guard and watch all that night. The next morning we espied a boat coming off from one of the pinnaces. So standing upon our guard, we hales them, and understood that Sir Thomas Gates and Sir George Somers were come in those pinnaces, which by their great industry they had builded in the Bermudas with the remainder of their wrecked ship and other wood they found in the country, upon which news we received no small joy, requesting them in the boat to come ashore, the which they refused and returned aboard again. For Sir Thomas Gates, having no knowledge of any fort to be builded there, was doubtful whether we were friends or no. But being possessed of the truth, he and Sir George Somers with divers others did come ashore at Algernon's Fort, and the next tide went up to Jamestown, where they might read a lecture of misery in our people's faces, and perceive the scarcity of victuals, and understand the malice of the savages, who, knowing our weakness, had divers times assaulted us without the fort, finding of five hundred men we had only left about sixty, the rest being either starved through famine or cut off by the savages. And those which were living were so meager and lean that it was lamentable to behold them, for many through extreme hunger have run out of their naked beds, being so lean that they looked like anatomies [skeletons], crying out, "We are starved, We are starved"; others, going to bed as we imagined in health, were found dead the next morning. And amongst the rest, one thing happened which was very remarkable, wherein God showed his just judgement. For one Hugh Pryse, being pinched with extreme famine, in a furious distracted mood did come openly into the market place blaspheming, exclaiming and crying out that there was no God, alleging that if there were a God he would not suffer his creatures whom he had made and framed to endure those miseries and to perish for want of foods and sustenance. But it appeared the same day that the Almighty was displeased with him, for going that afternoon with a butcher— a corpulent fat man—into the woods to seek for some relief, both of them were slain by savages.[5] And after being found, God's indignation was showed upon Pryse's corpse, which was rent in pieces with wolves or other wild beasts, and his bowels torn out of his body, being a lean, spare man; and the fat butcher, not lying above six yards from him, was found altogether untouched, only by the savages' arrows whereby he received his death.

These miseries considered, it was resolved upon by Sir Thomas Gates and the whole colony, with all speed to return for England, whereupon most of our men were set to work— some to make pitch and tar for trimming of our ships, others to bake bread, and few or none not employed in one occasion or another. So that (in) a small space of time four pinnaces were fitted and made ready. All preparing to go aboard, and if Sir

Thomas Gates had not labored with our men, they had set the town on fire, using these or the like words unto them, "My masters, let the town stand. We know not but that as honest men as ourselves may come and inhabit here." Then all of us embarking ourselves, Sir Thomas Gates in the *Deliverance* with his company, Sir George Somers in the *Patience*, myself in the *Discovery*, and Captain Davies in the *Virginia*. All of us sailing down the river with a full intent to have proceeded upon our voyage for England, when suddenly we espied a boat making towards us, wherein we found to be Captain Bruster sent from my Lord la Warr, who was come unto us with many gentlemen of quality and three hundred men, besides great store of victuals, munition, and other provision. Whereupon we all returned to Jamestown again, where my Lord shortly after landed and set all things in good order, selecting a council and making captains over fifty men apiece. Then Sir Thomas Gates, being desirous for to be revenged upon the Indians at Kecoughtan, did go thither by water with a certain number of men and, amongst the rest, a taborer [piper] with him. Being landed he caused the taborer to play and dance, thereby to allure the Indians to come unto him, the which prevailed. And then espying a fitting opportunity, fell in upon them, put five to the sword, wounded many others, some of them being after found in the woods with such extraordinary large and mortal wounds that it seemed strange they could fly so far. The rest of the savages he put to flight. And so possessing himself of the town and the fertile ground there unto adjacent, having well ordered all things, he left his Lieutenant Earley to command his company, and then returned to Jamestown again and shortly after did take his voyage for England. My Lord General about this time sent Captain Howldcrofte to build a fort in the woods near unto

Kecoughtan. The which being finished, my Lord named the same Charles Fort in honor of our King's Majesty that now is.[6]

Also my Lord sent Sir George Somers and Captain Argall in two ships into the Bermudas to make provision of hogs and fish for us. Sir George arrived there, where shortly after he died. His men, making good profit of ambergris and other commodities, returned for England. But Captain Argall, failing of the place, fell to the northward, where he happened upon some fish there, which having salted and dried, returned therewith to us to Jamestown again. . . .

NOTES

1. Percy, George, "A Trewe Relacyon," (Richmond: *Tyler's Quarterly Historical and Genealogical Magazine*, Volume III, no. 2, 1922), 259-70.

2. Wertenbaker, Thomas Jefferson, *Virginia Under the Stuarts, 1607-1608* (Princeton: Princeton University Press, 1914), 1.

3. Thirteen/WNET New York, *Secrets of the Dead*: "Death at Jamestown," 2002. http://www.pbs.org/wnet/secrets/case_jamestown/index.html.

4. Algernon was the oldest son of Percy's brother Henry.

5. How a "corpulent fat man" remained corpulent and fat in Jamestown in 1609 is unexplained.

6. In 1610 James I's son Charles was the Duke of York. By the time Percy wrote *A True Relation* in 1625, James I had died and Charles I had taken the throne.

PART IV

Beyond the Palisades

1610-1613

Tempest and Redemption

From

A True Reportory of the wrack, and redemption, of Sir Thomas Gates, Knight, upon and from the islands of the Bermudas: his coming to Virginia, and the estate of that colony then, and after, under the government of the Lord La Warr, July 15, 1610,

written by William Strachey, Esquire.[1]

The wreck of the Sea Venture *caused more deaths in Jamestown than on the ship itself. All of the* Sea Venture's *150 passengers and crew (and one dog) reached the sands of Bermuda safely, although their ship, wedged between two rocks just offshore, was a complete loss.*

William Strachey was one of those passengers. A second-generation gentleman (his father having acquired enough property in Westminster and Essex to receive a heraldic coat of arms), Strachey was traveling to Virginia in an attempt to remake his fortune. Educated at

Cambridge, and a member of Gray's Inn, Strachey was a shareholder in a theater company called the Children of Her Majesty's Revels, which owned the Blackfriars theater and employed the literary services of Ben Jonson and John Marston. His involvement in the theater makes it very likely that Strachey was at least an acquaintance of Shakespeare's; whether he was or not, Shakespearean scholars since the late eighteenth century have surmised that the Bard somehow saw a copy of Strachey's A True Reportory . . . and used it as the genesis for The Tempest.[2]

A True Reportory . . . is addressed to an unnamed "noble lady." It describes the wreck of the Sea Venture and the survivors' subsequent stay on Bermuda, where they built houses, planted gardens, and set the ship's carpenters to work building two pinnaces out of the native trees and what they could salvage from the Sea Venture (clearly, Jamestown needed these people). The Bermuda castaways were on the island for less than a year; as soon as the two pinnaces, named the Deliverance and the Patience, were sea-worthy, the 150 (and, presumably, the dog) boarded and set sail for Virginia. On arriving, more than a few probably wished they had stayed with their gardens on Bermuda.

The excerpt below is taken from the version collected and edited by Samuel Purchas (See Introduction on page xiv). The first part describes the hazardous escape from Bermuda and the disheartening landing at Jamestown, as well as the timely arrival of Lord de la Warr that saved the Virginia colony from abandonment. The second part is one of the most detailed physical descriptions of

*Jamestown itself, as well as a reasoned analysis of why
such a poor location was chosen in the first place.*

From this time we only awaited a favorable westerly wind
to carry us forth, which longer than usual now kept at the east,
and southeast, the way we were to go. The tenth of May early,
Sir George Somers and Captain Newport went off with their
long boats, and with two canoes boyed the channel, which we
were to lead it out in, and which was no broader from shoals on
the one side and rocks on the other than about three times the
length of our pinnace. About ten of the clock, that day being
Thursday, we set sail an easy gale, the wind at south, and by
reason no more wind blew, we were fain to tow her with our
longboat, yet neither with the help of that were we able to fit
our bows, but even when we came just upon them, we struck a
rock on the starboard side, over which the bow rode, and had it
not been a soft rock, by which means she bore it before her, and
crushed it to pieces, God knows we might have been like enough
to have returned anew and dwelt there, after ten months of
carefulness and great labor a longer time; but God was more
merciful unto us. When she struck upon the rock, the coxwain,
one Walsingham, being in the boat with a quick spirit (when
we were all amazed, and our hearts failed) and so by God's
goodness we led it out at three fathom, and three fathom and a
half water. The wind served us easily all that day and the next,
when (God be ever praised for it) to the no little joy of us all,
we got clear of the islands. After which holding a southerly
course, for seven days we had the wind sometimes fair, and
sometimes scarce and contrary; in which time we lost Sir George

Somers twice, albeit we still spared him our main topsail, and sometimes our fore-course too.

The seventeenth of May we saw change of water, and had much rubbish swim by our ship side, whereby we knew we were not far from land. The eighteenth about midnight we sounded, with the dipsing lead, and found thirty-seven fathom. The nineteenth, in the morning, we sounded, and had nineteen and a half fathom, stony, and sandy ground. The twentieth, about midnight, we had a marvelous sweet smell from shore . . . strong and pleasant, which did not a little glad us. In the morning, by daybreak (so soon as one might well see from the fore-top), one of the sailors descried land. . . .

This is the famous Chesapeake Bay, which we have called (in honor of our young prince) Cape Henry over against which within the Bay lyeth another headland, which we called in honor of our princely Duke of York, Cape Charles; and these lie northeast and by east, and southwest and by west, and they may be distant each from the other in breadth seven leagues, between which the sea runs in as broad as between Queensborough and Lee. Indeed it is a goodly bay, and a fairer, not easily to be found.

The one and twentieth, being Monday in the morning, we came up within two miles of Point Comfort, when the captain of the fort discharged a warning piece at us, whereupon we came to an anchor, and sent off our longboat to the fort, to certify who we were; by reason of the shoals which lie on the south side, this fort easily commands the mouth of the river, albeit it is as broad as [the Thames] between Greenwich and the Isle of Dogs.

True it is, such who talked with our men from the shore, delivered how safely all our ships the last year . . . arrived, and how our people (well increased) had therefore builded this fort;

only we could not learn any thing of our longboat, sent from the Bermudas, but what we gathered by the Indians themselves, especially from Powhatan, who would tell our men of such a boat landed in one of his rivers, and would describe the people, and make much scoffing sport thereat. By which we have gathered that it is most likely how it arrived upon our coast, and not meeting with our river, were taken at some time or other, at some advantage, by the savages, and so cut off. When our skiff came up again, the good news of our ships and men's arrival the last year did not a little glad our Governor, who went soon ashore, and as soon (contrary to all our fair hopes) had new unexpected, uncomfortable, and heavy news of a worse condition of our people above at Jamestown.

Upon Point Comfort our men did the last year (as you have heard) raise a little fortification, which since hath been better perfected, and is likely to prove a strong fort, and is now kept by Captain James Davies with forty men, and hath to name Algernon Fort, so called by Captain George Percy, whom we found at our arrival president of the colony, and at this time likewise in the fort. When we got into the point, which was the one and twentieth of May, being Monday about noon, where riding before an Indian town called Kecoughtan, a mighty storm of thunder, lightning, and rain, gave us a shrewd and fearful welcome.

From hence in two days (only by the help of tides, no wind stirring) we plied it sadly up the river, and the three and twentieth of May we cast anchor before Jamestown, where we landed, and our much grieved governor first visiting the church caused the bell to be rung, at which (all such as were able to come forth of their houses) repaired to church where our minister Master Buck made a zealous and sorrowful prayer, finding all things so contrary to our expectations, so full of misery and misgovernment. After service our governor caused me to read his commission, and Captain Percy (then president) delivered up unto him his commission, the old patent, and the council seal. Viewing the fort, we found the pallisadoes torn down, the ports open, the gates from off the hinges, and empty houses (which owners death had taken from them) rent up and burnt, rather than the dwellers would step into the woods a stone's cast off from them, to fetch other firewood. And it is true, the Indian killed as fast without, if our men stirred but beyond the bounds of their blockhouse, as famine and pestilence did within; with many more particularities of their sufferances (brought upon them by their own disorders the last year) than I have heart to express. In this desolation and misery our governor found the condition and state of the colony, and (which added more to his grief) no hope how to amend it or save his own company, and those yet remaining alive, from falling into the like necessities. For we had brought from the Bermudas no greater store of provision (fearing no such accidents possible to befall the colony here) than might well serve one hundred and fifty for a sea voyage; and it was not possible, at this time of the year to amend it, by an help from the Indian. For besides that they (at their best) have little more than from hand to mouth, it was now likewise but their seed-time, and all their corn scarce put into the ground. Nor was there at the fort . . . any means to take fish, neither sufficient seine, nor other convenient net, and yet if there had, there was not one eye of sturgeon yet come into the river. All which considered, it pleased our governor to make a speech unto the company, giving them to understand, that what provision he had, they should equally share with him, and if he should find it not possible, and easy to supply them with some thing from the country, by the endeavors of his able men, he would make ready, and transport them all into their native country (accomodating them the best that he could) at which there was a general acclamation, and shout of joy on both sides, for even our own men began to be disheartened and faint, when they saw this misery amongst the others, and no less threatened unto themselves. In the mean while, our governor published certain orders and instructions, which he enjoined them strictly to observe, the time that he should stay amongst them, which being written out fair, were set up upon a post in the church for every one to take notice of. . . .

Here (worthy Lady) let me have a little of your pardon, for having now a better heart than when I first landed, I will briefly describe unto you the situation and form of our fort. When Captain Newport in his first voyage did not like to inhabit upon so open a road as Cape Henry, nor Point Comfort, he plied it up to the river, still looking out for the most apt and securist place, as well for his company to sit down in, as which might give the least cause of offence or distaste, in his judgement, to the inhabitants. At length, after much and weary search . . . in the country of a werowance called Wowinchopunck (a ditionary [vassal] to Powhatan) within this fair river of Paspahegh, which we have called the King's River, a country least inhabited by the Indian, as they all the way observed, and three score miles and better up the fresh channel from Cape Henry, they had sight of an extended plain and spot of earth, which thrust out into the depth and middest of the channel, making a kind of . . . peninsula, for it was fastened only to the land with a slender neck, no broader than a man may well quaite [throw] a tile shard, and no inhabitants by seven or six miles near it. The trumpets sounding, the admiral struck sail, and before the same, the rest of the fleet came to an anchor, and here (as the best yet offered unto their view, supposed so much the more convenient, by how much with their small company, they were like enough the better to assure it) to lose no further time, the colony disembarked, and every man brought his particular store and furniture, together with the general provision ashore; for the safety of which, as likewise for their own security, ease, and better accomodating, a certain canton and quantity of that little half island of ground was measured, which they began to fortify, and thereon in the name of God to raise a fortress, with the ablest and speediest means they could. Which fort, growing since to more perfection, is now at the present in this manner.

A low level of ground about half an acre . . . on the north side of the river, is cast almost into the form of a triangle, and . . . pallizadoed. The south side, next to the river (howbeit extended in a line or curtain six score foot more in length than the other two, by reason the advantage of the ground doth so require), contains one hundred and forty yards, the west and east sides a hundred only. At every angle or corner, where the lines meet, a bulwark or watchtower is raised, and in each bulwark a piece of ordinance or two—well mounted. To every side, a proportioned distance from the pallisado, is a settled street of houses that runs along, so as each line of the angle hath his streets. In the middest is a market place, a storehouse, and a corps de guard, as likewise a pretty chapel, though (at this time when we came in) as ruined and unfrequented but the Lord Governor, and Captain General, hath given order for the repairing of it, and at this instant, many hands are about it. It is in length threescore foot, in breadth twenty-four, and shall have a chancel in it of cedar, and a communion table of the black walnut, and all the pews of cedar, with fair broad windows, to shut and open as the weather shall occasion, of the same wood, a pulpit of the same, with a font hewn hollow, like a canoe, with two bells at the west end. It is so cast as it be very light within, and the Lord Governor and Captain General doth cause it to be kept passing sweet and trimmed up with divers flowers, with a sexton belonging to it, and in it every Sunday we have sermons twice a day, and every Thursday a sermon, having true preachers, which take their weekly turns, and every morning at the ringing of a bell, about ten of the clock, each man addresseth himself to prayers, and so at four of the clock before supper. Every Sunday, when the Lord Governor and Captain General goeth to church, he is accompanied with all the councillors, captains, other officers, and all the gentlemen, and with a guard of halberdiers in his Lordship's livery, fair red cloaks, to the number of fifty, both on each side, and behind him; and being in the church, his Lordship hath his seat in the choir, in a green velvet chair, with a cloth, with a velvet cushion spread on a table before him on which he kneeleth, and on each side sit the council, captains, and officers, each in their place, and when he returneth home again, he is waited on to his house in the same manner.

And thus enclosed, as I said, round with a pallizado of planks and strong posts, four feet deep in the ground, of young oaks, walnuts, etc. The fort is called in honor of his Majesty's name, Jamestown; the principal gate from the town, through the pallizado, opens to the river, as at each bulwark there is a gate likewise to go forth, and at every gate a demi-culverin, and so in the marketplace. The houses first raised were all burnt by a casualty of fire the beginning of the second year of their seat, and in the second voyage of Captain Newport, which since have been better rebuilded, though as yet in great uniformity, either for the fashion or beauty of the street. A delicate wrought fine kind of mat the Indians make, with which (as they can be trucked for, or snatched up) our people do dress their chambers and inward rooms, which make their houses so much the more handsome. The houses have wide and large country chimnies in the which it is to be supposed (in such plenty of wood) what fires are maintained. And they have found the way to cover their houses, now (as the Indians) with barks of trees, as durable and as good proof against storms and winter weather as the best tile, defending likewise the piercing sunbeams of summer, and keeping the inner lodgings cool enough, which before in sultry weather would be like stoves, whilest they were, as at first, pargetted and plastered with bitumen or tough clay. And thus armed for the injury of changing times and seasons of the year, we hold ourselves well apaid, though wanting arras hangings, tapestry, and guilded Venetian cordovan, or more spruse household garniture, and wanton city ornaments. . . .

True it is, I may not excuse this our fort, or Jamestown, as yet seated in somewhat an unwholesome and sickly air, by reason it is in a marsh ground, low, flat to the river, and hath no fresh water springs serving the town, but what we drew from a well six or seven fathom deep, fed by the brackish river oozing into it, from whence I verily believe, the chief causes have proceeded of many diseases and sicknesses which have happened to our people, who are indeed strangely afflicted with fluxes and agues; and every particular season (by the relation of the old inhabitants) hath his particular infirmity too, all which (if it had been our fortunes to have seated upon some hill, accomodated with fresh springs and clear air, as do the natives of the country) we might have, I believe, well escaped. And some experience we have to persuade ourselves that it may be so, for of four hundred and odd men, which were seated at the Falls, the last year when the fleet came in with fresh and young able spirits, under the government of Captain Francis West, and of one hundred to the seawards (on the south side of our river) in the country of the Nansemonds, under the charge of Captain John Martin, there did not so much as one man miscarry, and but very few or none fall sick, whereas at Jamestown, the same time, and the same months, one hundred sickened, and half the number died. Howbeit, as we condemn not Kent in England for a small town called Plumstead, continually assaulting the dwellers there (especially newcomers) with agues and fevers, no more let us lay scandal and imputation upon the country of Virginia, because the little quarter wherein we are set down (unadvisedly so chosed) appears to be unwholesome, and subject to many ill airs, which accompany the like marsh places. . . .

NOTES

1. Purchas, Samuel, *Haklutus Posthumus, or Purchas his Pilgrimes* (London: Imprinted for Henry Fetherston at the sign of the rose in Paul's church yard, 1625), 1747-53.

2. Hume, Ivor Noel, *The Virginia Adventure: Roanoke to James Towne, An Archaeological and Historical Odyssey* (Charlottesville: University Press of Virginia, 1994), 243.

Laws Divine, Moral and Martial

From

Articles, Laws, and Orders, Divine, Politique, and Martial, for the Colony in Virginia: first established by Sir Thomas Gates, Knight, Lieutenant General, the 24th of May, 1610. Exemplified and approved by the Right Honorable Sir Thomas West, Knight, Lord la Warr, Lord Governor and Captain General, the 12th of June, 1610. Again exemplified and enlarged by Sir Thomas Dale, Knight, Marshall, and Deputy Governor, the 22nd of June, 1611.[1]

A society's body of laws reflects that society's concerns and fears. Virginia in 1610 had a lot of concerns and fears. Readers will hear, in many of these Laws Divine, Moral and Martial, *[although this abbreviated reference to the primary source differs slightly from the original title, this is the wording used during*

contemporary times] echoes of episodes from the
preceding narratives.

Laws also reflect a society's aspirations, though, and
this document shows the determination of Gates, Lord
de la Warr, and the Virginia Company to turn Jamestown
into a lasting and thriving community through the
rigorous implementation of martial law. Given the
colonists' past performance, such iron-fisted discipline
may have seemed entirely necessary.

Primarily concerned with religious orthodoxy, the
discipline of the military and labor forces, and regulation
of trade and commerce, the laws were articulated and
recorded by Strachey, who had become secretary of the
colony not long after his arrival in Virginia.

To the Right Honorable, the Lords of the Council of
Virginia. . . . By him, all whose duty is tributary to your
Lordships, and unto so excellent a cause,

William Strachey. . . .

Whereas his Majesty, like himself a most zealous Prince,
hath in his own realms a principal care of true religion, and
reverence to God, and hath always strictly commanded his
generals and governors, with all his forces wheresoever, to let
their ways be like his ends, for the glory of God—

And forasmuch as no good service can be performed, or
war well managed, where military discipline is not observed, and
military discipline cannot be kept where the rules or chief parts
thereof be not certainly set down, and generally known, I have
(with the advice and counsel of Sir Thomas Gates, Knight,

Lieutenant General) adhered unto the laws divine, and orders politique, and martial of his Lordship (the same exemplified) an addition of such others, as I have found either the necessity of the present state of the colony to require, or the infancy and weakness of the body thereof as yet able to digest, and do now publish them to all persons in the colony, that they may as well take knowledge of the Laws themselves, as of the penalty and punishment, which without partiality shall be inflicted upon the breakers of the same.

article 1.1

First, since we owe our highest and supreme duty, our greatest, and all our allegiance to Him, from whom all power and authority is derived, and flows as from the first and only fountain, and being especial soldiers empressed in this sacred cause, we must alone expect our success from Him, who is only the blesser of all good attempts, the King of kings, the commander of commanders, and Lord of Hosts, I do strictly command and charge all captains and officers, of what quality or nature soever, whether commanders in the field, or in the town, or towns, forts or fortresses, to have a care that the Almighty God be duly and daily served, and that they call upon their people to hear sermons, as that also they diligently frequent morning and evening prayer themselves by their own exemplar and daily life, and duty herein, encouraging others thereunto, and that such who shall often and willfully absent themselves be duly punished according to the martial law in that case provided.

article 1.2

That no man speak impiously or maliciously against the

holy and blessed Trinity, or any of the three persons, that is to say, against God the Father, God the Son, and God the Holy Ghost, or against the known articles of the Christian faith, upon pain of death.

article 1.3

That no man blaspheme God's holy name upon pain of death, or use unlawful oaths, taking the name of God in vain, curse . . . upon pain of severe punishment for the first offence so committed, and for the second, to have a bodkin [small dagger] thrust through his tongue, and if he continue the blaspheming of God's holy name, for the third time so offending, he shall be brought to a martial court, and there receive censure of death for his offence.

article 1.4

No man shall use any traitorous words against his Majesty's person or royal authority upon pain of death. . . .

article 1.6

Every man and woman . . . twice a day, upon the first tolling of the bell, shall upon the working days repair unto the church, to hear divine service, upon pain of losing his or her day's allowance for the first omission, for the second to be whipped, and for the third to be condemned to the galleys for six months. Likewise no man or woman shall dare to violate or break the Sabbath by any gaming, public or private, abroad or at home, but duly sanctify and observe the same, both himself and his family, by preparing themselves at home with private prayer, that they may be the better fitted for the public, according to the commandements of God, and the orders of our church, as also every man and woman shall repair in the morning to the divine service, and sermons preached upon the Sabbath day, and in the afternoon to divine service, and catechising, upon pain for the first fault to lose their provision, and allowance for the whole week following, for the second to lose the said allowance, and also to be whipped, and for the third to suffer death.

article 1.7

All preachers or ministers within this our colony, or colonies, shall in the forts where they are resident, after divine service, duly preach every Sabbath day in the forenoon, and catechise in the afternoon, and weekly say the divine service, twice every day, and preach every Wednesday; likewise every minister where his is resident, within the same fort, or fortress, towns or town, shall choose unto him four of the most religious and better disposed, as well to inform of the abuses and neglects of the people in their duties, and service to God, as also to the due reparation, and keeping of the church handsome, and fitted with all reverent observances thereunto belonging. Likewise every minister shall keep a faithful and true record, or church book, of all christenings, marriages, and deaths of such our people as shall happen within their fort, or fortresses, towns or town at any time, upon the burden of a neglectful conscience, and upon pain of losing their entertainment.

article 1.8

He that upon pretended malice shall murder or take away the life of any man shall be punished with death.

article 1.9

No man shall commit the horrible and detestable sins of sodomy upon pain of death, and he or she that can be lawfully convicted of adultery shall be punished with death. No man shall ravish or force any woman, maid or Indian or other, upon pain of death, and know ye that he or she that shall commit fornication, and evident proof made thereof, for their first fault shall be whipped, for their second they shall be whipped, and for their third shall be whipped three times a week for one month, and ask public forgiveness in the assembly of the congregation. . . .

article 1.12

No manner of person whatsoever shall dare to detract, slander, calumniate, or utter unseemly and unfitting speeches, either against his Majesty's honorable council for this colony, resident in England, or against the committees, assistants unto the said council, or against the zealous endeavors and intentions of the whole body of adventurers for this pious and Christian plantation, or against any public book or books, which by their mature advice, and grave wisdoms, shall be thought fit to be set forth and published for the advancement of the good of this colony and the felicity thereof, upon pain for the first time so offending, to be whipped three several times [on three separate occasions, not with just three lashes], and upon his knees to acknowledge his offence and to ask forgiveness upon the Sabbath day in the assembly of the congregation, and for the second time so offending to be condemned to the galley for three years, and for the third time so offending to be punished with death.

article 1.13

No manner of person whatsoever, contrary to the word of God (which ties every particular and private man, for conscience sake, to obedience and duty of the magistrate, and such as shall be placed in authority over them) shall detract, slander, calumniate, murmur, mutiny, resist, disobey, or neglect the commandments either of the Lord Governor and Captain General, the Lieutenant General, the Marshall, the council, or any authorized captain, commander, or public officer, upon pain for the first time so offending to be whipped three several times, and upon his knees to acknowledge his offence, with asking forgiveness upon the Sabbath day in the assembly of the congregation, and for the second time so offending to be condemned to the galley for three years, and for the third time so offending to be punished with death.

article 1.14

No man shall give any disgraceful words, or commit any act to the disgrace of any person in this colony, or any part thereof, upon pain of being tied head and feet together upon the guard [in the corps de guard] every night for the space of one month, besides to be publicly disgraced himself, and be made incapable ever after to possess any place or execute any office in this employment.

article 1.15

No man of what condition soever shall barter, truck, or trade with the Indians, except he be thereunto appointed by lawful authority, upon pain of death.

article 1.16

No man shall rifle or despoil, by force or violence, take away anything from any Indian coming to trade, or otherwise, upon pain of death.

article 1.17

No Cape Merchant, or Provant Master, or Munition Master, or Truck Master, or keeper of any store, shall at any time embezzle, sell, or give away anything under his charge to any favorite . . . more than unto any other, whom necessity shall require in that case to have extraordinary allowance of provisions, nor shall they give a false account unto the Lord Governor and Captain General, unto the Lieuetenant General, unto the Marshall, or any deputed governor at any time having the command of the colony, with intent to defraud the said colony, upon pain of death. . . .

article 1.19

There shall no captain, master, mariner, sailor, or any else of what quality or condition soever, belonging to any ship or ships, at this time remaining, or which shall hereafter arrive within this our river, bargain, buy, truck, or trade with any one member in this colony, man, woman, or child, for any tool or instrument of iron, steel or what else, whether appertaining to smith, carpenter, joiner, shipwright, or any manual occupation, or handicraft man whatsoever, resident within our colony. Nor shall they buy or bargain for any apparel, linen or woolen, household stuff, bed, bedding, sheet, towels, napkins, brass, pewter, or such like, either for ready money, or provisions. Nor shall they exchange their provisions, of what quality soever, whether butter, cheese, biscuit, meal, oatmeal, aquavite, oil, bacon, any kind of spice, or such like, for any such aforesaid instruments, or tools, apparel, or household stuff, at any time, or so long as they shall here remain from the date of these presents, upon pain of loss of their wages in England, confiscation and forfeiture of such their monies and provisions, and upon peril beside of such corporal punishment as shall be inflicted upon them by verdict and censure of a martial court. Nor shall any officer, soldier, or tradesman, or any else of what sort soever, members of this colony, dare to sell any such tool or instruments, necessary and useful for the business of the colony, or truck, sell, exchange, or give away his apparel or household stuff of what sort soever, unto any such seaman, either for money, or any such foresaid provisions, upon pain of three times several whipping, for the one offender, and the other upon peril of incurring censure, whether of disgrace, or addition of such punishment as shall be thought fit by a court martial.

article 1.20

Whereas sometimes heretofore, the covetous and wide affections of some greedy and ill disposed seamen, sailors, and mariners, laying hold upon the advantage of the present necessity under which the colony sometimes suffered, have sold unto our people provisions of meal, oatmeal, biscuit, butter, cheese, etc., at unreasonable rates and prices unconscienable. For avoiding the like to be now put in practice, there shall no captain, master, mariner, or sailor, or what officer else belonging to any ship or ships now within our river, or hereafter which shall arrive, shall dare to bargain, exchange, barter, truck, trade, or sell, upon pain of death, unto any . . . member of this present colony, any provisions of what kind soever above the determined valuations and prices set down and proclaimed and sent therefore unto each of your several ships, to be fixed upon your main mast, to the intent that want of due notice, and ignorance in this case, be no excuse, or plea, for any one offender herein. . . .

article 1.22

There shall no man or woman, launderer or launderess, dare to wash any unclean linen . . . or throw out the water or suds of foul clothes, in the open street, within the pallizadoes, or within forty foot of the same, nor wrench and make clean any kettle, pot, or pan, or such like vessel within twenty foot of the old well or new pump. Nor shall any one aforesaid, within less than a quarter of one mile from the pallizadoes, dare to do the necessities of nature, since by these unmanly, slothful, and loathsome immodesties, the whole fort may be choked and poisoned with ill airs, and so corrupt (as in all reason cannot but much infect the same). And this shall they take notice of, and avoid, upon pain of whipping and further punishment as shall be thought meet by the censure of a martial court. . . .

article 1.25

Every man shall have an especial and due care to keep his house sweet and clean, as also so much of the street as lieth before his door, and especially he shall so provide and set his bedstead whereon he lieth, that it may stand three foot at least from the ground, as he will answer the contrary at a martial court.

article 1.26

Every tradesman in their several occupation, trade, and function, shall duly and daily attend his work upon his said trade or occupation, upon peril for his first fault, and negligence therein, to have his entertainment checked for one month, for his second fault three month, for his third one year, and if he continue still unfaithful and negligent therein, to be condemned to the galley for three years. . . .

article 1.28

No soldier or tradesman but shall be ready, both in the morning and in the afternoon, upon the beating of the drum, to go out unto his work. Nor shall he return home, or from his work, before the drum beat again, and the officer appointed for that business bring him of, upon peril for the first fault to lie upon the guard head and heels together all night, for the second time so faulting to be whipped, and for the third time so offending to be condemned to the galleys for a year.

article 1.29

No man or woman (upon pain of death) shall run away from the colony to Powhatan, or any savage werowance else whatsoever. . . .

article 1.32

Whosoever seaman or landman of what quality, or in what place of command soever, shall be employed upon any discovery, trade, or fishing voyage into any of the rivers within the precincts of our colony, shall for the safety of those men who are committed to his command stand upon good and careful guard for the prevention of any treachery in the

Indian; and if they touch upon any shore, they shall be no less circumspect and wary, with good and careful guard day and night, putting forth good sentinel, and observing the orders and discipline of watch and ward; and when they have finished the discovery, trade, or fishing, they shall make haste with all speed, with such bark or barks, pinnace, galley, ship, etc., as they shall have the command of, . . . to Jamestown again, not presuming to go beyond their commission, or to carry any such bark or barks, galley, pinnace, ship, etc., for England or any other country in the actual possession of any Christian prince, upon peril to be held an enemy to this plantation, and traitor thereunto, and accordingly to lie liable unto such censure of punishment (if they arrive in England) as shall be thought fit by the Right Honorable Lords, his Majesty's Council for this colony, and if it shall so happen, that he or they shall be prevented, and brought back hither again into the colony, their treacherous flight to be punished with death.

article 1.33

There is not one man nor woman in this colony now present, or hereafter to arrive, but shall give up an account of his and their faith and religion, and repair unto the minister, that by his conference with them, he may understand and gather whether heretofore they have been sufficiently instructed and catechised in the principles and grounds of religion, whose weakness and ignorance herein, the minister finding, and advising them in all love and charity, to repair often unto him, to receive therein a greater measure of knowledge. If they shall refuse so to repair unto him, and he the minister give notice thereof unto the governor, or that chief officer of that town or fort, wherein he or she, the parties so offending, shall remain, the governor shall cause the offender for his first time of refusal to be whipped, for the second time to be whipped twice, and to acknowledge his fault upon the Sabbath day, in the assembly of the congregation, and for the third time to be whipped every day until he hath made the same acknowledgement, and asked forgiveness for the same, and shall repair unto the minster to be further instructed as aforesaid; and upon the Sabbath when the minister shall catechise, and of him demand any question concerning his faith and knowledge, he shall not refuse to make answer upon the same peril. . . .

article 1.36

No man or woman whatsoever, members of this colony, shall sell or give unto any captain, mariner, master, or sailor, etc., any commodity of this country, of what quality soever, to be transported out of the colony for his or their own private uses, upon pain of death.

Every minister or preacher shall every Sabbath day, before catechising, read all these laws and ordinances publicly in the assembly of the congregation, upon pain of his entertainment checked for that week.

Article 2 . . .

article 2.3

If any soldier, or what manner of man else soever, of what quality or condition soever he be, shall tacitly compact with any seaman, captain, master, or mariner to convey himself aboard any ship, with intent to depart from and abandon the colony, without a lawful pass from the General, or chief commander of the colony, at that time, and shall happen to be prevented, and taken therewith, before the ship shall depart out of our bay, that captain, master, or mariner that shall so receive him, shall lose his wages, and be condemned to the galleys for three years, and he the sworn servant of the colony, soldier, or what else, shall be put to death with the arms which he carrieth.

article 2.4

When any select and appointed forces, for the execution and performance of any intended service, shall be drawn into the field, and shall dislodge from one place unto another, that soldier that shall quit or forsake his colors shall be punished with death. . . .

article 2.8

He that shall begin a mutiny shall be put to death with such arms as he carrieth. . . .

article 2.20

He that shall swagger, and give injurious words upon the court of guard, for the first offence, he shall ask forgiveness upon his knees, of the officers, and rest of the guard, before the captain of the watch at that time; for his second time so offending, he shall be committed to the galleys for one year. . . .

article 2.22

He that should draw his sword in a town of garrison, or in a camp, shall lose his right hand. . . .

article 2.34

That soldier who, fighting with an enemy, shall lose his arms, or run away cowardly, or yield himself but upon apparent and great constraints, or without having performed first the part of a good soldier and an honest man, shall suffer death with the arms which he carrieth. . . .

article 2.37

That soldier which upon an assault, or taking of any town, that shall not follow his colors, and the victory, but shall fall to pillage for his private profit, after the place taken, shall suffer death with the arms which he weareth.

article 2.38

No soldier may speak or have any private conference with any of the savages, without leave of his captain, nor his captain without leave of his chief officer, upon pain of death. . . .

article 2.41

No soldier shall unprofitably waste his powder, shot, or match by shooting it idly away, or at birds, beasts, or fowl, but shall give an account unto his corporal of the same, who shall certify his captain upon peril for his first fault so committed to be committed to prison, there to lie in irons head & heels together eight and forty hours, for the second to the condemned six months to the galleys, and for the third offence to be condemned two years to the galleys. . . .

article 2.44

Whosoever shall give offense to the Indians in that

nature, which truly examined, shall found to have been cause
of breach of their league and friendship, which with so great
travail, desire, and circumspection we have or shall at any time
obtain from them, without commission so to do from him
that hath authority for the same, shall be punished with death.

article 2.45

Whosoever shall willfully or negligently set fire on any
Indian dwelling house . . . or temple, or upon any storehouse,
or garner of grain, or provision of what quality soever . . .
ransack, or ill entreat the people of the country, where any
war, or where through any march shall be made except it be
proclaimed, or without commandment of the chief officers,
shall be punished with death. . . .

article 2.47

Whosoever shall fain himself sick upon the point of fight,
or when any work is to be done, or slip away from the service
of either, shall be punished by death.

article 2.48

Whosoever shall raise any question, brabble or brawl in
the watch, or ambuscado, or in scout, or sentinel in any other
effect, or make any noise or rumor where silence, secrecy, and
covert is to be required, shall be punished with death. . . .

article 2.51

Every captain shall cause to be read all these laws which
concern martial discipline, every week upon his guard day,
unto his company upon pain of censure of a martial court.

NOTE

1. Force, Peter, *Tracts and Other Papers Relating Principally to the origin, settlement, and progress of the colonies in North America, from the Discovery of the country to the year 1776* (Washington: Printed by Peter Force, 1836-46), 9-36.

Sir Thomas Dale and the First Four Towns

From

A True Discourse of the Present Estate of Virginia, and the success of the affairs there till the 18th of June, 1614, together with a relation of the several English towns and forts, the assured hopes of that country, and the peace concluded with the Indians, the christening of Powhatan's daughter and her marriage with an Englishman, written by Ralph Hamor the younger, late secretary in that colony.[1]

> *Sir Thomas Dale arrived in Virginia in May 1611, after a brief and uneventful crossing. An experienced soldier, Dale was sent to serve as marshal to the governor-general, Lord de la Warr. But the governor had left the colony in March, suffering from one of the many*

illnesses that afflicted the Jamestown settlers. Though he had been appointed governor for life, and intended to return to England just long enough to recover his health, he instead stayed seven years, and died trying to reach Virginia again.

In Lord de la Warr's absence, Dale took over. He expanded the written laws of the colony, turning them into more of a martial than a civil code. He and his men started the colonists on a variety of construction projects, both within and without the pallisades of Jamestown. He encouraged the explorations and trading of Captain Samuel Argall (see "The Capture of Pocahontas," also from Hamor's True Discourse, *on pages 224-31). He dealt aggressively enough with the Indians that he felt safe founding a few plantations and three new towns— Henrico and Bermuda City up the James from the peninsula, and Kecoughtan down the river near its mouth. Dale also instituted new policies for the management of land grants and supplies from the common store.*

Ralph Hamor arrived in Virginia with Lord de la Warr in 1610, and was named one of two clerks of the council. His True Discourse *was written shortly after his return to England in 1614; although Hamor writes as an unabashed advocate for Virginia, his narrative lacks the personal biases and self-serving tone of George Percy's or John Smith's.*

The many publications and impressions of Virginia, an employment wherein to this day myself and many other unstaid heads . . . have been too unprofitably engaged, might justly excuse my silence, did not the filial duty, whereby in all things to the utmost of my power I am bound to obey my father, compel me unwillingly thereunto: a task I know by himself and others, merely because I have been *oculatus testis* [eyewitness], thus imposed upon me, in the undertaking and performance whereof, I heartily wish that my poor relation, rich only in truth (as I shall clearly justify myself by eyewitnesses also) may give any credit or encouragement to proceed in a business so full of honor, and worth, whereunto (if there were no secondary causes) the already published ends, I mean the glory of God, in the conversion of those infidels, and the honor of our King and country (which by right may claim at the least their superfluities, from those whom God hath in this world made his dispensers and purse-bearers) might be a sufficient spur to resolved Christians, especially the state and condition of our colony, so standing when I left it, and I assure myself in this time grown more mature, that an honest heart would even relent, and mourn to think how poorly, I dare not say unworthily, it is prosecuted. It being true that now after five years' intestine war with the revengeful, implacable Indians, a firm peace (not again easily to be broken) hath been lately concluded, not only with the neighbor and bordering Indians, as on Patawomeke, Tappahanna, and other rivers, but even with that subtle old revengeful Powhatan and all the people under his subjection, for all whom Powhatan himself stands firmly engaged, by which means we shall not only be furnished with what commodities their country yieldeth, and have all the helps they may afford us in our endeavors (as they are easily taught, and may lenity and fair usage, as Sir Thomas Dale now principal commander there, and most worthy the honor he holds, is well experienced in their dispositions, and accordingly makes use of them) be brought, being naturally though ingenious, yet idly given, to be no less industrious, nay to exceed our English, especially those which we hitherto and as yet are furnished with, who for the most part no more sensible then beasts, would rather starve in idleness (witness their former proceedings) than feast in labor, did not the law compel them thereunto, but also which will be most for our benefit, our own men may without hazard, I might say with security (by self-experience) follow their several labors, whereby twenty shall now be able to perform more than heretofore hath been forty.

Though I conjecture and assure my self that ye cannot be ignorant by what means this place hath been thus happily, both for our proceeding and the welfare of the naturals, concluded, yet for the honor of Captain Argall, whose endeavors in the action entitled him most worthy, I judge it no whit impertinent in my discourse to insert them, which with as much brevity as I may, not omitting the circumstances most pertinent and material, I shall endeavor. . . .

The greatest, and many enemies and disturbers of our proceedings, and that which hath hitherto deterred our people to address themselves into those parts, have been only two: enmity with the naturals, and the bruit of famine. One of these two (and that indeed, which was some cause of the other) I have already removed, and shall as easily take away the other. Howbeit, it were too great folly (I might say impudency in me) to aver that there hath reigned no such infection in the colony, occasioned merely by misgovernment, idleness, and faction, and chiefly by the absence of the ever worthy commanders, Sir

Thomas Gates, and Sir George Somers, by the providence of God, miraculously wrecked and saved upon the hopeful Somer Islands, since myself cannot but witness, of which I had some taste in what a miserable condition we found the colony at our arrival there from the Bermudas, not living above threescore persons therein, and those scarce able to go alone, of well nigh six hundred, not full ten months before. Yet now I dare and will boldly affirm to the greatest adversary of the plantation, that shall aver the contrary, that there is that plenty of food, which every man by his own industry may easily, and doth procure that the poorest there, and most in want, hath not been so much pinched with hunger this four years that if he would take any pains, he knew not where to fetch a good meal's meat. And true it is, that every day by the providence and blessing of God, and their own industry, they have more plenty than other the reason hereof is at hand, for formerly, when our people were fed out of the common store and labored jointly in the manuring of the ground, and planting corn, glad was that man that could slip from his labor, nay the most honest of them in a general business would not take so much faithful and true pains in a week, as now he will do in a day. Neither cared they for the increase, presuming that howsoever their harvest prospered, the general store must maintain them, by which means we reaped not so much corn from the labors of 30 men, as three men have done for themselves. To prevent which mischief hereafter, Sir Thomas Dale hath taken a new course throughout the whole colony, by which means the general store (apparel only excepted) shall not be charged with any thing. . . . He hath allotted, to every man in the colony, three English acres of clear corn ground, which every man is to mature and tend, being in the nature of farmers, (the Bermuda undertakers only excepted) and they are not called unto any service or labor belonging to the colony more then one month in the year, which shall neither be in seed time, or in harvest, for which, doing no other duty to the colony, they are yearly to pay into the store two barrels and a half of corn, there to be reserved to keep new men, which shall be sent over, the first year after their arrival.[2] And even by these means, I dare say, our store will be bountifully furnished, to maintain three or four hundred men, whensoever they shall be sent thither to us. That money which hitherto hath been disbursed to provide a twelve months' victuals, if there were but now half so much bestowed in clothes, and bedding, will be such comfort to the men, as even thereby the lives of many shall not only be preserved, but also themselves kept in strength and heart, able to perform such businesses as shall be imposed upon them. And thus shall also the former charge be well saved, and yet more business effected, the action reknowned, and more commodity returned to the Merchant, and yet faint for want of encouragement.

Concerning the undertaking of the Bermuda City, a business of greatest hope ever begun in our territories there, their patent, which I purpose in this treatise to insert, doth apparently demonstrate upon what terms and conditions they voluntarily have undertaken that employment. How forward that business is, in his due place shall be expressed, only give me leave with as much brevity as I may, lest any man should divert his mind, and be fearful to adventure his person thither, for fear of famine and penury, to amplify a little the plenty there. For if it be true, as most certain it is, that those whom I have described under the title of farmers can pay into our store two barrels and a half of corn yearly, and others who labor eleven months in the general business of the colony, and but one to provide themselves victuals, why should any man (if he be industrious) mistrust starving? If otherwise, for any part, and I think all that are engaged in the action, and understand the business, accord with me herein, and would not with his company there, nay they shall much wrong themselves, and the action, if they do not withstand such, and deny them passage. For even they and none else have been the occasions of the manifold imputations and disgraces which Virginia hath innocently undergone through their defaults. I would, therefore, by these relations not only encourage honest and industrious, but also deter all lazy, impotent, and ill livers from addressing themselves thither, as being a country too worthy for them and altogether disconsonant to their natures, which must either brook labor or hazard, and undergo much displeasure, punishment, and penury, if they escape a thing which few idlers have done, the scurvy disease, with which few, or none once infected, have recovered.

To proceed, therefore, in my encouragement to painful people, such as either through . . . in this world, or wrecked rents, or else great charge of children and family, live here [in England], and that not without much care and sweat, into extreme poverty: for those, this country hath present remedy. Every such person, so well disposed to adventure thither, shall soon find the difference between their own and that country. The affairs in the colony, being so well ordered, and the hardest tasks already overpast, that whosoever (now, or hereafter) shall happily arrive there, shall find a handsome house of some four rooms or more, if he have a family, to repose himself in rent free, and 12 English acres of ground adjoining thereunto, very strongly impaled, which ground is only allotted unto him for roots, garden herbs, and corn. Neither shall he need to provide himself, as were wont the first planters, of a year's provision of victuals, for that the store there will be able to afford him. And upon these conditions he shall be entertained: he shall have, for himself and family, a competent 13 months' provision delivered unto him, in which time it must be his care to provide for himself and family ever after, as those already there. To this end he shall be furnished with necessary tools of all sorts, and for his better subsistence he shall have poultry, and swine, and, if he deserve it, a goat or two, perhaps a cow given him, which, once compast, how happily he may live, as do many there, who I am sure will never return. . . .

In May 1611, Sir Thomas Dale, with a prosperous passage . . . arrived there, with him about three hundred people, such as for the present speed and dispatch could then be provided, of worse condition than those formerly there, who, I sorrow to speak it, were not so provident, though once before bitten with hunger and penury, as to put corn into the ground for their winter's bread, but trusted to the store, then furnished but with eight months provision. His first care, therefore, was to employ all hands about setting of corn at the two forts seated upon Kecoughtan, Henry and Charles, whereby the season then not fully past, though, about the end of May, we had there an indifferent crop of good corn.

This business taken order for, and the care and trust of it committed to his under officers, to Jamestown he hastened, where the most company were, and the daily and usual workers, bowling in the streets. These he employed about necessary works, as felling of timber, repairing their houses ready to fall upon their heads, and providing pales, posts, and rails to impale his purposed new town, which, by reason of his ignorance in those parts, but newly arrived there, he had not resolved where to seat. For his better knowledge therefore of those parts, himself with a hundred men spent some time in discovery, first Nansemond River, which in despite of the Indians, then our enemies, he discovered to the head. After that, our own river to the falls, whereupon a high land environed with the main river, some fifteen or twenty miles from the head of the falls, near to an Indian town called Arsateck, he resolved to plant his new town, and so did, whereof in his due place shall I make a brief relation.

It was no mean trouble to him to reduce his people so timely to good order, being of so ill a condition as may well witness his severe and strict imprinted book of articles, then needful with all severity and extremity to be executed, now much mitigated, for more deserved death in those days than do now the least punishment. So as if the law should not have restrained by execution, I see not how the utter subversion and ruin of a colony should have been prevented . . . So as Sir Thomas Dale hath not been tyrranous, nor severe at all; indeed, the offences have been capital, and the offenders dangerous, incurable members, for no use so fit as to make examples to others. But the manner of their death, may some object, hath been cruel, unusual and barbarous, which indeed they have not been. . . . What if they have been more severe then usual in England; there was just cause for it. We were rather to have regard to those whom we would have terrified, and made fearful to commit the like offences, than to the offenders justly condemned, it being true that amongst those people (who for the most part are sensible only . . . of the body's torment) the fear of a cruel, painful, and unusual death more restrains them than death itself.

Thus much . . . I proceed in his endeavors . . . which was only in preparing timber, pales, posts, and rails for the present impaling this new town to secure himself and men from the malice and treachery of the Indians, in the midst and heart of whom he was resolved to set down. But before he could make himself ready for that business, Sir Thomas Gates, though his passage more long than usual, to second him herein, happily arrived about the second of August with six good ships, men, provisions, and cattle, whom, as yet not fully discovered, we supposed to be a Spanish fleet . . . It did me much good, and gave great courage to the whole company, to see the resolution of Sir Thomas Dale, now wholly busied (our land forrications too weak to withstand a foregn enemy) in lading our provisions aboard the two good ships, the *Star* and *Prosperous*, and our own *Deliverance*, then riding before Jamestown; aboard which ships he had resolved to encounter the supposed enemy, animating his people not only with the hope of victory if they readily obeyed his direction, but also assuring them that if by these means God had ordained to set a period to their lives, they could never be sacrificed in a more acceptable service, himself promising rather to fire the Spanish ships with his own than either basely to yield or to be taken. And in nothing he seemed so much discontent as that we could not possibly lade aboard all our provisions before (the wind being then very fair) they might have been with us. Whilst, therefore, the rest were laboring their utmost to lade aboard our provisions, he caused a small shallop to be manned with thirty ready and good shot to discover directly what ships they might be, and with all speed to return him certain word, which within three hours they did, assuring him that it was an English fleet, Sir Thomas Gates General thereof. Which news, how welcome it was unto him, principally because now he doubted not the happy progression of the affairs in hand. . . .

The worthies being met, after salutation and welcome given, and received, Sir Thomas Dale acquainted Sir Thomas Gates both with such businesses as he had affected since his arrival, and also of his resolutions to build a new town at the falls, which design and purpose of his, Sir Thomas Gates, then principal governor in Virginia, well approving, furnished him with three hundred and fifty men, such as himself made choice of. . . . The beginning of September, 1611, he set from Jamestown, and in a day and a half landed at a place where he purposed to seat and build, where he had not been ten days before he had very strongly impaled seven English acres of ground for a town, which in honor of the noble Prince Henry (of ever happy and blessed memory, whose royal heart was ever strongly affected to that action) he called by the name of Henrico. No sooner was he thus fenced, and in a manner secured from the Indians, but his next work (without respect to his own health or particular welfare) was building, at each corner of the town, very strong and high commanders or watchtowers, a fair and handsome church, and storehouses; which finished, he began to think upon convenient houses and lodging for himself and men, which with as much speed as was possible were, more strongly and more handsome than any formerly in Virginia, contrived and finished . . . even in four months space, he had made Henrico much better and of more worth than all the work ever since the colony began. . . .

I should be so tedious if I should give up the account of every day's labor, which therefore I purposely omit, and will only describe the town in the very state and perfection which I left it. . . . First, for the situation, it stands upon a neck of a very high land, three parts thereof environed with the main river [the James], and cut over between the two rivers [actually a bend in the James] with a strong pale, which maketh the neck of land an island. There is in this town three streets of well framed houses, a handsome church, and the foundation of a more stately one laid of brick, in length a hundred foot, and fifty foot wide; besides storehouses, watchhouses, and such like. There are also, as ornaments belonging to this town, upon the verge of this river, five fair blockhouses, or commanders, wherein live the honester sort of people, as in farms in England, and there keep continual sentinel for the town's security. . . . About two miles from the town into the main, a rail of two miles in length, cut over from river to river, guarded likewise with several commanders, with a great quantity of corn ground impaled, sufficient, if there were no more in the colony secured, to maintain with but easy manoring and husbandry. . . .

For the further enlargement yet of this town, on the other side of the river . . . is secured to our use, especially for our hogs to feed in, about twelve English miles of ground, by name, Hope in Faith, Coxen Dale, secured by five forts. . . . Here hath Mr. Whittaker chosen his parsonage, or church land, some hundred acres impaled, and a fair framed parsonage house built thereupon, called Rock Hall of this town, and all the forts thereunto belonging hath Captain James Davies the principal command and government.

I proceed to our next and most hopeful habitation, whether we respect commodity, or security . . . against foreign designs and invasions. I mean the Bermuda City, begun about Christmas last, which because it is the nearest adjoining to Henrico, though the last undertaken, I hold it pertinent to handle in the next place. This town or plantation is seated by land some five miles from Henrico, by water, fourteen. Being the year before the habitation of the Appomattoc, to revenge the treacherous injury of those people done unto us, taken from them, besides all their corn, the former before without the loss of any, save only some few of those Indians. . . . At what time Sir Thomas Dale, being himself upon that service, and duly considering how commodious a habitation and seat it might be for us, took resolutions to possess and plant it, and at that very instant gave it the name of the new Bermudas, whereunto he hath laid out and annexed, to be belonging to the freedom and corporation forever, many miles of champion [fields] and woodland, in several hundreds, as the Upper and Nether Hundreds, Rochdale Hundred, West Shirley Hundred, and Digges his Hundred. In the Nether Hundred he first began to plant and inhabit, for that there lieth the most convenient quantity of corn ground, and with a pale cut over from river to river, about two miles long, we have secured some eight miles circuit of ground, the most part champion, and exceeding good corn ground. Upon which pale, and round about, upon the verge of the river in this Hundred, half a mile distant from each other are very fair houses already builded, besides divers other particular men's houses, not so few as fifty, according to the conditions of the patent granted them. . . . In this plantation, next to Sir Thomas Dale, is principal in the command Captain George Yeardley, Sir Thomas Gates his lieutenant, whose endeavors have ever deserved worthy commendations in that imployment. Rochdale Hundred, by a cross pale well nigh four miles long, is also already impaled, with bordering houses all along the pale; in which Hundred our hogs and other cattle have twenty miles' circuit to graze in securely. The undertaking of the chief city [is] deferred till their harvest be in, which, once reaped, all hands shall be employed thereon, which Sir Thomas Dale purposeth, and he may with some labor effect his designs, to make an impregnable retreat against any foreign invasion, how powerful so ever.

About fifty miles from this seat, on the other side of the river, is Jamestown situated, upon a goodly and fertile island. Which, although formerly scandalled with unhealthful air, we have since approved as healthful as any other place in the country. And this I can say by mine own experience, that that corn and garden ground (which with much labor being have cleared, and impaled) is as fertile as any other we have had experience and trial of. The town itself, by the care and providence of Sir Thomas Gates, who for the most part had his chiefest residence there, is reduced into a handsome form, and hath in it two fair rows of houses, all of framed timber, two stories, and an upper garret or corn loft . . . besides three large and substantial storehouses, joined together in length some hundred and twenty foot, and in breadth forty. And this town hath been lately newly and strongly impaled, and a fair platform for ordinance in the west bulwark raised. There are also without this town, in the island, some very pleasant and beautiful houses; two blockhouses, to observe and watch lest the Indians at any time should swim over the back river, and come into the island; and certain other farm houses. The command and government of this town hath master John Scarpe, lieutenant to Captain Francis West, brother to the right honorable, the Lord de la Warr.

From Jamestown downwards, some forty and odd miles, at the mouth of the river, near Point Comfort, upon Kecoughtan, are two pleasant and commodious forts, Henry and Charles, goodly seats, and much corn ground about them, abounding with the commodities of fish, fowl, deer, and fruits, whereby the men live there, with half that maintenance out of the store which in other places is allowed. Certainly this habitation would be no whit inferior to the best we have there, save, as yet, with the poor means we have, we cannot secure it, if a foreign enemy, as we have just cause to expect daily, should attempt it. And of these forts, Captain George Webb was lately established the principal commander.

NOTES

1. Hamor, Ralph, *A True Discourse of the Present Estate of Virginia* (London: Printed at London by John Beale for William Welby, dwelling at the sign of the Swanne in Paul's church yard, 1615), 16-34.

2. The Bermuda referred to here is Bermuda Nether Hundred, a plantation up the river from Jamestown.

A Spy in Virginia

From
Letter of Don Diego de Molina[1]
1613

> *In the summer of 1611, a single caravel weighed anchor off Point Comfort and three men came ashore. Ambushed and captured by Captain James Davies, the commander for Algernon's Fort, the leader of the men turned out to be Don Diego de Molina, described by George Percy as the commander of a West Indies fort. Molina explained to Davies that his ship had been blown off course, and offered to stay on shore with his own pilot if an English pilot could be provided to steer his ship safely to anchorage. Davies, being an Englishman,*

considered this a sporting request and complied. The Spanish caravel promptly sailed away, leaving Molina and the Spanish pilot, who was soon suspected of being an Englishman gone into the service of Spain.[2]

Molina remained in Jamestown until 1616, when he was taken to England by Captain Samuel Argall (on the same ship that carried Sir Thomas Dale). Molina used his time as a prisoner at Jamestown to make careful observations about the fort and the garrison guarding it, many of which, like this one, he managed to smuggle back to Spain. Just as the English in the New World lived in constant fear of the Spanish attack that Molina calls for here, so the Spanish nursed the memory of English pirates like Raleigh and Drake; Molina fears Jamestown not as the first step in territorial conquest, but as a base for pirates. His descriptions provide an interesting counterpoint to the more positive observations of Ralph Hamor and William Strachey. Molina thought little of Jamestown's defenses, whether the pallisade surrounding the town or the forts at the mouth of the James. He describes the colonists' morale as extremely low, suggesting that the Laws Divine, Moral and Martial and the strict discipline of Dale were not as appreciated as Hamor believed.

The person who will give this to your Lordship is very trustworthy, and your Lordship can give credence to everything he will say, so I will not be prolix in this but will tell in it what is most important. Although with my capture and the extraordinary occurrences following it his Majesty will have opened his eyes and seen this new Algiers of America, which is coming into existence here, I do not wonder that in all this time he has not remedied it because to effect the release would require an expedition, particularly as he lacks full information for making a decision.[3] However I believe that with the aid of your Lordship's intelligence and with the coming of the caravel to Spain, his Majesty will have been able to determine what is most important and that that is to stop the progress of a hydra in its infancy, because it is clear that its intention is to grow and encompass the destruction of all the West, as well by sea as by land and that great results will follow I do not doubt, because the advantages of this place make it very suitable for a gathering-place of all the pirates of Europe, where they will be well received. For this nation has great thoughts of an alliance with them. And this nation by itself will be very powerful because as soon as an abundance of wheat shall have been planted and there shall be enough cattle, there will not be a man of any sort whatever who will not alone or in company with others fit out a ship to come here and join the rest, because as your Lordship knows this kingdom [England] abounds in poor people who abhor peace—and of necessity, because in peace they perish—and the rich are so greedy and selfish that they even cherish a desire for the Indies and the gold and silver there—notwithstanding that there will not be much lack of these here, for they have discovered some mines which are considered good, although they have not yet been able to derive profit from them. But when once the preliminary steps are taken there are many indications that they will find a large number in the mountains. So the Indians say and they offer to show the locations that they know and they say that near the sources of the rivers, as they come down from the mountain, there is a great quantity of grains of silver and gold, but, as they do not set any value on these but only on copper which they esteem highly, they do not gather them.

As yet these men have not been able to go to discover these although they greatly desire it, nor to pass over this range to New Mexico and from there to the South Sea where they expect to establish great colonies and fit out fleets with which to become lords of that sea as well as of this, by colonizing certain islands among those to the east of the channel of Bahama and even to conquer others, as Puerto Rico, Santo Domingo and Cuba. And although this would be difficult at the least, we have already seen signs of these purposes in the colonizing of Bermuda where they are said to have strong fortifications, because the lay of the land is such that a few can defend themselves against a great number and prevent disembarking and landing. . . .

The soil in this place is very fertile for all species, only not for those which require much heat, because it is cold. There is much game and fish, but as they have not begun to get profit from the mines, but only from timber, the merchants have not been able to maintain this colony with as much liberality as was needed and so the people have suffered much want, living on miserable rations of oats or maize and dressing poorly. For which reason, if today three hundred men should come, this same year would destroy more than one hundred and fifty, and there is not a year when half do not die. Last year there were seven hundred people and not three hundred and fifty remain, because little food and much labor on public works kills them and, more than all, the discontent in which they live seeing themselves treated as slaves with cruelty. Wherefore many have gone over to the Indians, at whose hands some have been killed, while others have gone out to sea, being sent to fish, and those who remain have become violent and are desirous that a fleet should come from Spain to take them out of their misery. Wherefore they cry to God of the injury that they receive and they appeal to his Majesty in whom they have great confidence, and should a fleet come to give them passage to that kingdom, not a single person would take up arms. Sooner would they forfeit their respect and obedience to their rulers who think to maintain this place till death.

And although it is understood there [Spain] that the merchants [of the London Company] are deserting this colony, this is false for it is a strategem with which they think to render his Majesty careless, giving him to understand that this affair will settle itself, and that thus he will not need to go to the expense of any fleet whatever to come here. With eight hundred or one thousand soldiers he could reduce this place with great ease, or even with five hundred, because there is no expectation of aid from England for resistance and the forts which they have are of boards and so weak that a kick would break them down, and once arrived at the ramparts those without would have the advantage over those within because its beams and loopholes are common to both parts—a fortification without skill and made by unskilled men. Nor are they efficient soldiers, although the rulers and captains make a great profession of this because of the time they have served in Flanders on the side of Holland, where some have companies and castles. The men are poorly drilled and not prepared for military action.

However they have placed their hope on one of two settlements, one which they have founded twenty leagues up the river in a bend on a rugged peninsula with a narrow entrance by land and they are persuaded that there they can defend themselves against the whole world. I have not seen it but I know that it is similar to the others and that one night the Indians entered it and ran all over the place without meeting any resistance, shooting their arrows through all the doors, so that I do not feel that there would be any difficulty in taking it or the one in Bermuda, particularly if my advice be taken in both matters as that of a man who has been here two years and has considered the case with care. I am awaiting his Majesty's decision and am desirous of being of some service and I do not make much of my imprisonment nor of the hardships which I have suffered in it, with hunger, want and illness, because one who does a labor of love holds lightly all his afflictions. The ensign Marco Antonio Perez died fifteen months ago, more from hunger than illness, but assuredly with the patience of a saint and the spirit of a good soldier. I have not fared very ill, but tolerably so, because since I arrived I have been in favor with these people and they have shown me friendship as far as their own wretchedness would allow, but with genuine good-will. The sailor who came with me is said to be English and a pilot. He declares that he is from Aragon and in truth no one would take him for a foreigner.[4]

This country is located in thirty-seven and a third degrees, in which is also the bay which they call Santa Maria.[5] Five rivers empty into this, very wide and of great depth—this one at its entrance nine fathoms and five and six within. The others measure seven, eight and twelve; the bay is eight leagues at its mouth but in places it is very wide, even thirty leagues. There is much oak timber and facilities for making ships, trees for them according to their wish—very dark walnut which they esteem highly and many other kinds of trees.

The bearer is a very honorable Venetian gentleman, who having fallen into some great and serious errors is now returned to his first religion and he says that God has made me his instrument in this, for which I give thanks. He wishes to go to Spain to do penance for his sins. If I get my liberty I think of helping him in everything as far as I shall be able. I beseech your Lordship to do me the favor of making him some present, for I hold it certain that it will be a kindness very acceptable to our Lord to see in your Lordship indications that charity has not died out in Spain. And so your Lordship ought to have charity and practice it in the case of a man who goes from here poor and sick and cannot make use of his abilities, and if I have to stay here long I am no less in need of your Lordship's help (as you will learn from the report of this man, who will tell you how I am faring). Your Lordship might aid me by sending some shipstores such as are brought here for certain private individuals and in particular cloth and linen for clothing ourselves (this man and me) because we go naked or so ragged that it amounts to the same, without changing our shirts in a month, because, as the soldier says, my shirts are an odd number and do not come to three. I trust in God who will surely help me since He is beginning to give me my health which for eleven months has failed me. I have not sufficient opportunity to write to his Majesty. Your Lordship will be able to do this giving him notice of everything I am telling. May God guard your Lordship as I desire. From Virginia, May 28, 1613.

If your Lordship had the key to my cipher, I should write in it. But this letter is sewed between the soles of a shoe, so that I trust in God that I shall not have done wrong in writing in this way. When I first came here I wrote his Majesty a letter which had need of some interpretation and directed it with others to your Lordship. I do not know whether you have received them. . . .

NOTES

1. Tyler, Lyon Gardiner, *Narratives of Early Virginia, 1606-1625*, (New York: Charles Scribner's Sons, 1907), 218-24.

2. Hume, Ivor Noel, *The Virginia Adventure: Roanoke to James Towne, An Archaeological and Historical Odyssey* (Charlottesville: University Press of Virginia, 1994), 335. The pilot identified himself as Francisco Lembri, but was soon revealed to be Francis Limbrecke, who had been a pilot for Spain as far back as the 1588 Armada. The pilot left Virginia with Molina in 1616, but Argall waited to hang him by the ship's yardarm until they were within sight of the English coast.

3. Algiers was notorious as a base for pirates who plundered the Mediterranean and Atlantic.

4. Hume, 335.

5. The Chesapeake Bay

PART V

The Peace of Pocahontas

1614

The Capture of Pocahontas

from

A True Discourse of the Present Estate of Virginia, and the success of the affairs there till the 18th of June, 1614, together with a relation of the several English towns and forts, the assured hopes of that country, and the peace concluded with the Indians, the christening of Powhatan's daughter and her marriage with an Englishman, written by Ralph Hamor the younger, late secretary in that colony.[1]

Pocahontas may or may not have saved John Smith's head from the execution block, but her service to the Jamestown colony is unquestioned. Smith and other chroniclers describe her acting, even as a child, as an informal envoy from her father. Tradition held that she frequently brought corn and other gifts to the English compound, and seemed to be curious about and generous to the Jamestown colonists.[2] *Smith's* General History *claims that the girl went so far as to warn Smith about a trap her father had laid for him. In return for her kindness,* the English, specifically Captain Samuel Argall, tricked and kidnapped Pocahontas in 1613 (she was a teenager at the time), bringing her back to Jamestown to use her as a trump card in negotiations with her father. When Powhatan refused to ransom her, Pocahontas was kept at Henrico and instructed in the Christian faith. While in captivity she and an Englishman named John Rolfe apparently fell in love, and love was to accomplish what arms had not. The Peace of Pocahontas was inaugurated on her wedding day in 1614, and lasted until the 1622 massacre and subsequent retaliations, in which the Virginian English attacked and burned native villages throughout the Tidewater region.

Rolfe had been aboard the Sea Venture during its wreck and escape from Bermuda, finally arriving in Virginia in 1610. Though he later served as secretary, recorder-general, and councilor for the colony, his great contribution to Jamestown (other than marrying Pocahontas) was the successful introduction of a strain of West Indian tobacco far superior to the native variety (for more information, see "Sir Thomas Dale and the First Four Towns," pages 197-209). The cultivation of tobacco finally turned Virginia into a profitable venture.[3] This was not the first marriage for either Rolfe or Pocahontas. Rolfe's first wife crossed with him on the Sea Venture. Their daughter was born on Bermuda, but died before they left the island; his wife died sometime after their arrival in Virginia. Pocahontas had been married at puberty to one of Powhatan's warriors. No divorce proceedings took place when Powhatan approved his daughter's marriage with Rolfe, and the feelings of her soon-to-be-cast-off husband were not mentioned, if they were even noted.[4]

In 1615 the Rolfe's son Thomas was born. The following year the family arrived in England as living, breathing advertisements for the Virginia Company. In somebody's idea of cleverness, the Rolfes were lodged at the Belle Sauvage Inn near St. Paul's Cathedral. Pocahontas/Rebecca Rolfe was received—gawked at, more likely—at court (although her husband was not brought to court, either because of his low birth or because of his success with the tobacco James I so hated), where she watched a masque written by Ben Jonson.[5] She had a poignant reunion with John Smith, who had been trying in vain to persuade the Virginia Company to re-hire him. At some point in the winter of 1617, Pocahontas and her son Thomas fell ill. The Rolfes tried to return quickly to Virginia, but Pocahontas's condition significantly worsened before the ship could reach the sea reach of the Thames. She was taken ashore at Gravesend, where she died March 21, 1617.

Rolfe returned to Virginia, leaving Thomas in Plymouth until he was strong enough to cross. Rolfe continued to serve the colony until his death, apparently from natural causes, in 1622. Thomas Rolfe did return to Virginia in the late 1630s; at one point, his great-uncle Opechancanough nominated him to become chief of the Powhatan Empire. Rolfe remained a loyal servant of the Crown, serving as an officer in the militia, although he did successfully petition the governor to visit some of his mother's family. Many modern Americans can claim Pocahontas as an ancestor, thanks to the family founded by Thomas Rolfe.

The following excerpt from Hamor's A True
Discourse *describes Argall's kidnapping of Pocahontas
and Dale's subsequent attempts to force Powhatan's hand.*

The general letters, upon my knowledge, directed and sent
to the honorable Virginia Council, being most of them (though
myself most unworthy) by me penned, have intimated how that
the everworthy gentleman Captain Argall, in the heat of our home
furies and disagreements, by his best experience of the disposition
of those people, partly by gentle usage and partly by the
composition and mixture of threats, hath ever kept fair and
friendly quarter with our neighbors bordering on other rivers of
affinity, yea consanguinity, no less near than brothers to
Powhatan, such is his well known temper and discretion, yea to
this pass hath he brought them, and they assuredly trust upon
what he promiseth, and are as careful in performing their mutual
promises, as though they contended to make that maxim, that
there is no faith to be held with infidels, a mere and absurd
paradox. Nay as I have heard himself relate . . . they have even
been pensive and discontented with themselves, because they
knew not how to do him some acceptable good turn, which might
not only pleasure him, but even be profitable to our whole colony
and plantation, yea ever assuring him that when the times should
present occasion, they would take hold of her forelock and be
the instruments to work him content, and even thus they proved
themselves as honest performers as liberal promisers. It chanced
Powhatan's delight and darling, his daughter Pocahontas, (whose
fame hath even been spread in England by the title of
"Nonparrella of Virginia") in her princely progress, if I may so
term it, took some pleasure (in the absence of Captain Argall) to

be among her friends at Patawomeke (as it seemeth by the relation I had) employed thither, as shopkeepers to a fair, to exchange some of her father's commodities for theirs; where residing some three months or longer, it fortuned upon occasion, either of promise or profit, Captain Argall to arrive there, whom Pocahontas, desirous to renew her familiarity with the English, and delighting to see them, as unknown, fearful perhaps to be surprised, would gladly visit, as she did, of whom no sooner had Captain Argall intelligence, but he dealt with an old friend and adopted brother of his, Japazeus, how and by what means he might procure her captive, assuring him that now or never was the time to pleasure him, if he intended indeed that love which he had made profession of, that in ransom of her he might redeem some of our English men and arms now in the possession of her father, promising to use her withal fair and gentle. . . . Japazeus well assured that his brother, as he promised, would use her courteously, promised his best endeavors and secrecy to accomplish his desire, and thus wrought it, making his wife an instrument (which sex have ever been most powerful in beguiling enticements) to effect his plot which he had thus laid, he agreed that himself, his wife, and Pocahontas would accompany his brother to the water side, whether come, his wife should feign a great and longing desire to go aboard and see the ship, which being there three or four times before, she had never seen, and should be earnest with her husband to permit her. He seemed angry with her, making, as he pretended, so unnecessary a request, especially being without the company of women, which denial she taking unkindly, must fain to weep (as who knows not that women can command tears), whereupon her husband, seeming to pity those counterfeit tears, gave her leave to go aboard, so that it would please Pocahontas to accompany her.

Now was the greatest labor to win her, guilty perhaps of her father's wrongs, though not known as she supposed to go with her, yet by her earnest persuasions, she assented. So forthwith aboard they went, the best cheer that could be made was seasonably provided, to supper they went, merry on all hands, especially Japazeus and his wife, who to express their joy would ere be treading upon Captain Argall's foot, as who should say tis done, she is your own. Supper ended, Pocahontas was lodged in the gunners' room, but Japazeus and his wife desired to have some conference with their brother, which was only to acquaint him by what stratagem they had betrayed his prisoner, as I have already related; after which discourse, to sleep they went, Pocahontas nothing mistrusting this policy, who nevertheless being most possessed with fear, and desire of return, was first up, and hastened Japazeus to be gone. Captain Argall, having secretly well rewarded him with a small copper kettle and some other less valuable toys so highly by him esteemed that doubtless he would have betrayed his own father for them, permitted both him and his wife to return, but told him that for divers considerations, as for that his father had then eight of our Englishmen, many swords, pieces, and other tools, which he had at several times, by treacherous murdering our men, taken from them, which though of no use to him, he would not redeliver, he would reserve Pocahontas, whereat she began to be exceeding pensive, and discontented, yet ignorant of the dealing of Japazeus, who in outward appearance was no less discontented that he should be the means of her captivity, much ado there was to persuade her to be patient, which with extraordinary courteous usage, by little and little was wrought in her, and so to Jamestown she was brought, a messenger to her father forthwith dispatched to advertise him that his only daughter was in the hands and possession of the English, there to be kept till such times as he would ransom her with our men, swords, pieces, and other tools treacherously taken from us. The news was unwelcome, and troublesome unto him, partly for the love he bare to his daughter, and partly for the love he bare to our men his prisoners, of whom (though with us they were unapt for any employment) he made great use; and those swords, and pieces of ours (which though of no use to him), it delighted him to view, and look upon.

He could not, without long advice and deliberation with his council, resolve upon anything, and it is true, we heard nothing of him, till three months after, by persuasions of others, he returned us seven of our men, with each of them a musket unserviceable, and by them sent us word, that whensoever we pleased to deliver his daughter, he would give us, in satisfaction of his injuries done to us, and for the rest of our pieces broken and stolen from him, 500 bushels of corn, and be forever friends with us. The men and pieces in part of payment we received, and returned him answer that his daughter was very well, and kindly treated, and so should be howsoever he dealt with us. But we could not believe that the rest of our arms were either lost or stolen from him, and therefore, till he returned them all, we would not by any means deliver his daughter, and then it should be at his choice, whether he would establish peace, or continue enemies with us. This answer, as it seemed, pleased him not very well, for we heard no more from him till in March last, when with Captain Argall's ship and some other vessels belonging to the colony, Sir Thomas Dale with a hundred and fifty men well appointed, went up into his own river [the York], where his chiefest habitations were, and carried with us his daughter, either to move them to fight for her, if such were their courage and boldness, as hath been reported, or to restore the residue of our demands, which were our pieces, swords, tools. Some of the same men which he returned (as they promised) ran to him again. . . . A great bravado all the way as we went up the river they made, demanding the cause of our coming thither, which we told them was to deliver Pocahontas, whom purposely we had brought with us, and to receive our arms, men, and corn, or else to fight with them, burn their houses, take away their canoes, break down their fishing weirs, and do them what other damages we could. Some of them, to set a good face on the matter, replied that if we came to fight with them we were welcome, for they were provided for us, counseling us rather to retire (if we loved our safeties) than proceed; bragging, as well they might, that we had ever had the worst of them in that river, instancing by Captain Ratcliffe (not worthy remembering, but to his dishonor) who with most of his company they betrayed and murdered. We told them since they durst remember us of that mischief, unless they made the better and more speedy agreement, we would now revenge that treachery, and with this discourse by the way as we went, we proceeded, and had no sooner entered the narrow of the river, the channel there lying within shot of the shore, but they let their arrows fly amongst us in the ship, themselves unseen to us, and in the forehead hurt one of our men, which might have hazarded his life without the present help of a skillful surgeon.

Being thus justly provoked, we presently manned our boats, went ashore, and burned in that very place some forty houses, and of the things we found therein made freeboot and pillage, and as themselves afterward confessed unto us, hurt and killed five or six of their men. With this revenge satisfying ourselves for that their presumption in shooting at us, and so the next day proceeded higher up the river, and Indians calling unto us, and demanding why we went ashore, burned their houses, killed and hurt their men, and took away their goods. We replied that though we came to them in peaceable manner, and would have been glad to have received our demands with love and peace, yet we had hearts and power to take revenge, and punish where wrongs should be offered, which having now done, though not so severely as we might, we rested content therewith, and are ready to embrace peace with them if they pleased. Many excuses they seemed to pretend, that they shot not at us, but (if any such abuse were offered) it was some straggled Indian, ignorant of our pretence in coming to them, affirming that they themselves would be right glad of our love, and would endeavor to help us to what we came for, which being in the possession of Powhatan their King, they would without delay dispatch messengers to him, to know his purpose and pleasure, desiring fair quarter some 24 hours, for so long they pretend it would be before their messengers might return. This we granted, and what we promised, we ever exactly performed. The time now come, we inquired what Powhatan would do, and had for answer that our Englishmen lately with him, fearful to be put to death by us (see *Laws Divine, Moral and Martial*), were run away, and some of Powhatan's men sent abroad in quest of them, but our swords and pieces, so many as he had, should be brought the next day, which, merely to delay time, they bare us in hand. The next day they came not. Higher up the river we went, and anchored near unto the chiefest residency Powhatan had, at a town called Matchcot, where were assembled (which we saw) about 400 men, well appointed with their bows and arrows to welcome us. Here they dared us to come ashore, a thing which we purposed before, so ashore we went, our best landing being up a high steep hill which might have given the enemy much advantage against us, but it seemed they, as we, were unwilling to begin, and yet would gladly have been at blows, being landed as if they had no show of fear, they stirred not from us, but walked up and down, by and amongst us, the best of them inquiring for our Werowance or king, with whom they would gladly consult to know the occasion of our coming thither. . . .When they were informed, they made answer that they were there ready to defend themselves, if we pleased to assault them, desiring nevertheless some small time to dispatch two or three men once more to their king, to know his resolution, which if not answerable to our requests, in the morning, if nothing else but blood would then satisfy us, they would fight with us, and thereby determine our quarrel, which was but a further delay to procure time to carry away their provisions. Nevertheless we agreed to this their request, assuring them till the next day by noon we would not molest, hurt, nor detain any of them, and then, before we fought, our drum and trumpets should give them warning. Upon which promise of ours, two of Powhatan's sons, being very desirous to see their sister who was there present ashore with us, came unto us, at the sight of whom, and her well fare, whom they suspected to be worse treated, though they had often heard the contrary, they much rejoiced, and promised that they would undoubtedly persuade their father to redeem her, and to conclude a firm peace forever with us, and upon this resolution the two brothers with us retired aboard, we having first dispatched two Englishmen, Master John Rolfe and Master Sparkes, to acquaint their father with the business in hand. The next day, being kindly treated, they returned, not at all admitted [into] Powhatan's presence, but spake with his brother Apachamo, his successor, one who hath already the command of all the people, who likewise promised us his best endeavors to further our just requests. . . .We, because the time of the year being then April, called us to our business at home to prepare ground, and set corn for our winter's provisions, upon these terms departed, giving them respite till harvest to resolve what was best for them to do, with this proviso: that if final agreement were not made betwixt us before that time, we would thither return again and destroy and take away all their corn, burn all the houses upon that river, leave not a fishing weir standing, nor a canoe in any creek thereabout, and destroy and kill as many of them as we could.

Long before this time, a gentleman of approved behavior and honest carriage, master John Rolfe, had been in love with Pocahontas and she with him, which thing at the instant that we were in parley with them, myself made known to Sir Thomas Dale by a letter from him, whereby he entreated his advice and furtherance in his love, if so it seemed fit to him for the good of the plantation, and Pocahontas herself, acquainted her brethren therewith. Which resolution, Sir Thomas Dale well approving, was the only cause: he was so mild amongst them, who otherwise would not have departed their river without other conditions.

The bruit of this pretended marriage came soon to Powhatan's knowledge, a thing acceptable to him, as appeared by his sudden content thereunto, who some ten days after sent an old uncle of hers, named Opachisco [Opechancanough], to give her as his deputy in the church, and two of his sons to see the marriage solemnized, which was accordingly done about the fifth of April, and ever since we have had friendly commerce and trade, not only with Powhatan himself, but also with his subjects round about us; so as now I see no reason why the colony should not thrive apace.[6]

Notes

1. Hamor, Ralph, *A True Discourse of the Present Estate of Virginia* . . . (London: Printed at London by John Beale for

William Welby, dwelling at the sign of the Swanne in Paul's church yard, 1615), 3-11.

2. Hume, Ivor Noel, *The Virginia Adventure: Roanoke and James Towne, An Archaeological and Historical Odyssey* (Charlottesville: University Press of Virginia, 1994), 324.

3. Palmer, Alan and Veronica, *Who's Who in Shakespeare's England* (New York: St. Martin's Press, 1999), 206-7.

4. Rountree, Helen C., *The Powhatan Indians of Virginia* (Norman: University of Oklahoma Press, 1989), 91.

5. Hume, *The Virginia Adventure*, 337.

6. Hamor could have meant "intended" instead of "pretended" in the first sentence of this paragraph.

The Love Letter of John Rolfe

From
*A True Discourse of the Present Estate of Virginia, and the
success of the affairs there till the 18th of June, 1614, together
with a relation of the several English towns and forts, the
assured hopes of that country, and the peace concluded with
the Indians, the christening of Powhatan's daughter and her
marriage with an Englishman, written by Ralph Hamor the
younger, late secretary in that colony.*[1]

*This is the text of John Rolfe's letter to Sir Thomas
Dale, in which Rolfe announces his intentions to marry
Pocahontas and argues his case. If the language of this
letter strikes the reader as awfully legalistic for a man
head-over-heels in love, please remember that this*

version passed by two image-conscious editors—Ralph Hamor and Samuel Purchas—before publication.

Honorable Sir, and most worthy Governor:

When your leisure shall best serve you to peruse these lines, I trust in God, the beginning will not strike you into a greater admiration, than the end will give you good content. It is a matter of no small moment, concerning my own particular, which here I impart unto you, and which toucheth me so nearly, as the tenderness of my salvation. Howbeit I freely subject myself to your grave and mature judgement, deliberation, approbation, and determination; assuring myself of your zealous admonitions, and godly comforts, either persuading me to desist, or encouraging me to persist therein, with a religious fear and godly care, for which (from the very instant that this began to root itself within the secret bosom of my breast) my daily and earnest prayers have been, still are, and ever shall be produced forth with as sincere a godly zeal as I possibly may to be directed, aided and governed in all my thoughts, words, and deeds, to the glory of God, and for my eternal consolation. To persevere wherein I never had more need, nor (till now) could ever imagine to have been moved with the like occasion. . . .

But to avoid tedious preambles, and to come nearer the matter: first suffer me with your patience, to sweep and make clean the way wherein I walk from all suspicions and doubts, which may be covered therein, and faithfully to reveal unto you, what should move me hereunto.

Let therefore this my well advised protestation, which here I make between God and my own conscience, be a sufficient witness, at the dreadful day of judgement (when the secret of all men's hearts shall be opened) to condemn me herein, if my chiefest intent and purpose be not to strive, with all my power of body and mind, in the undertaking of so mighty a matter, no way led (so far forth as man's weakness may permit) with the unbridled desire of carnal affection; but for the good of this plantation, for the honor of our country, for the glory of God, for my own salvation, and for the converting to the true knowledge of God and Jesus Christ, an unbelieving creature, namely Pocahontas. To whom my hearty and best thoughts are, and have a long time been so entangled, and enthralled in so intricate a labyrinth, that I was even awearied to unwind myself thereout. But almighty God, who never faileth his that truly invocate his holy name, hath opened the gate, and led me by the hand that I might plainly see and discern the safe paths wherein to tread.

To you therefore (most noble sir), the patron and father of us in this country, do I utter the effects of this settled and long continued affection (which hath made a mighty war in my meditations) and here I do truly relate, to what issue this dangerous combat is come unto, wherein I have not only examined, but thoroughly tried and pared my thoughts even to the quick, before I could find any fit, wholesome, and apt applications to cure so dangerous an ulcer. I never failed to offer my daily and faithful prayers to God, for his sacred and holy assistance. I forgot not to set before mine eyes the frailty of mankind, his proneness to evil, his indulgence of wicked thoughts, with many other imperfections wherein man is daily ensnared, and oftentimes overthrown, and them compared to my present estate. Nor was I ignorant of the heavy displeasure which almighty God conceived against the sons of Levy and

Israel for marrying strange wives, nor of the inconveniences which may thereby arise, with other the like good motions which made me look about warily and with good circumspection, into the grounds and principal agitations, which thus should provoke me to be in love with one whose education hath been rude, her manners barbarous, her generation accursed, and so discrepant in all nurtriture from myself that oftentimes, with fear and trembling, I have ended my private controversy with this: surely these are wicked instigations, hatched by him who seeketh and delighteth in man's destruction; and so with fervent prayers to be ever preserved from such diabolical assaults (as I took those to be) I have taken some rest.

Thus when I had thought I had obtained my peace and quietness, behold another, but more gracious tentation hath made breaches into my holiest and strongest meditations, with which I have been put to a new trial, in a straighter manner than the former; for besides the many passions and sufferings which I have daily, hourly, yea and in my sleep endured, even awaking me to astonishment, taxing me with remissness, and carelessness, refusing and neglecting to perform the duty of a good Christian, pulling me by the ear, and crying: why dost not thou endeavor to make her a Christian? And these have happened to my greater wonder, even when she hath been furthest separated from me, which in common reason (were it not an undoubted work of God) might breed forgetfulness of a far more worthy creature. Besides, I say the holy spirit of God often demanded of me, why I was created? If not for transitory pleasures and worldly vanities, but to labor in the Lord's vineyard, there to sow and plant, to nourish and increase the fruits thereof, daily adding, with the good husband in the Gospel, somewhat to the talent, that in the end the fruits may be reaped to the comfort of the laborer in this life, and his salvation in the world to come? And if this be, as undoubtedly this is, the service Jesus Christ requireth of his best servant, woe unto him that hath these instruments of piety put into his hands and willfully despiseth to work with them. Likewise, adding hereunto her great appearance of love to me, her desire to be taught and instructed in the knowledge of God, her capableness of understanding, her aptness and willingness to receive any good impression, and also the spiritual, besides her own incitements stirring me up hereunto.

What should I do? Shall I be of so untoward a disposition as to refuse to lead the blind into the right way? Shall I be so unnatural as not to give bread to the hungry? Or uncharitable, as not to cover the naked? Shall I despise to actuate these pious duties of a Christian? Shall the base fears of displeasing the world overpower and withhold me from revealing unto man these spiritual works of the Lord, which in my meditations and prayers I have daily made known unto him? God forbid. . . .

Again by my reading, and conference with honest and religious persons, have I received no small encouragement, besides *serena mea conscientia*—the clearness of my conscience—clean from the filth of impurity, *quoe est instar muri ahenei*—which is unto me as a brazen wall. If I should set down at large the perturbations and godly motions which have striven within me, I should but make a tedious and unnecessary volume. But I doubt not these shall be sufficient both to certify you of my true intents, in discharging of my duty to God, and to yourself, to whose gracious providence I humbly submit myself, for His glory, your honor, our country's good, the benefit of this plantation, and for the converting of one unregenerate, to regeneration; which I beseech God to grant, for his dear son Christ Jesus his sake.

Now if the vulgar sort, who square all men's actions by the

base rule of their own filthiness, shall tax or taunt me in this my godly labor: let them know, it is not any hungry appetite, to gorge myself with incontinency; sure (if I would, and were so sensually inclined) I might satisfy such desire, though not without a seared conscience, yet with Christians more pleasing to the eye, and less fearful in the offense unlawfully committed. Nor am I in so desperate an estate that I regard not what becometh of me; nor am I out of hope but one day to see my country, nor so void of friends, nor mean in birth, but there to obtain a match to my great content; nor have I ignorantly passed over my hopes there, or regardlessly seek to lose the love of my friends, by taking this course. I know them all, and have not rashly overslipped any.

But shall it please God thus to dispose of me (which I earnestly desire to fulfill my ends before set down) I will heartily accept of it as a godly tax appointed me, and I will never cease (God assisting me) until I have accomplished, and brought to perfection, so holy a work, in which I will daily pray God to bless me, to mine and her eternal happiness. And thus desiring no longer to live, to enjoy the blessings of God, then this my resolution doth tend to such godly ends, as are by me before declared; not doubting of your favorable acceptance, I take my leave, beseeching Almighty God to rain down upon you such plenitude of his heavenly graces as your heart can wish and desire, and so I rest,

At your command most willing to be disposed of,
John Rolfe

NOTE

1. Hamor, Ralph, *A True Discourse of the Present Estate of*

Virginia . . . (London: Printed at London by John Beale for William Welby, dwelling at the sign of the Swanne in Paul's church yard, 1615), 61-68.

The Last Mission to Powhatan

From

A True Discourse of the Present Estate of Virginia, and the success of the affairs there till the 18th of June, 1614, together with a relation of the several English towns and forts, the assured hopes of that country, and the peace concluded with the Indians, the christening of Powhatan's daughter and her marriage with an Englishman, written by Ralph Hamor the younger, late secretary in that colony.[1]

> Not satisfied with the Peace of Pocahontas, in the spring of 1614 Sir Thomas Dale sent Ralph Hamor and Thomas Savage to visit Powhatan in his capital of Matchcot, near what is now Richmond, to ask for the

hand of another of Powhatan's daughters in marriage—
to Dale. The fiancée-to-be was only twelve years old,
which is less scandalous than the fact that Sir Thomas
had a Lady Dale waiting for him back in England, to
whom he would return in about two years.[2] Hamor's
account of his visit includes Powhatan's eloquent and
sorrowful farewell to the English, to whom he seems to
concede the land that had once been his. As he promised,
Powhatan withdrew further from the new Virginians,
leaving most of the running of his empire to his brothers
Opitchapam and Opechancanough. Powhatan died in
April 1618.

I purposely omitted one thing in the treatise of our concluded peace, where with I intend to conclude my discourse, which already I have drawn to a longer period than I purposed, whereby we have gathered the better assurances of their honest inward intentions, and this it is.

It pleased Sir Thomas Dale (myself being much desirous, before my return for England, to visit Powhatan and his court, because I would be able to speak somewhat thereof by mine own knowledge) to employ myself and an English boy for my Interpreter, one Thomas Savage (who had lived three years with Powhatan, and speaks the language naturally; one whom Powhatan much affecteth), upon a message unto him, which was to deal with him if by any means I might procure a daughter of his, who (Pocahontas being already in our possession) is generally reported to be his delight, and darling, and surely he esteemeth her as his own soul, for surer pledge of peace.[3]

I departed the fifteenth of May, early in the morning, with

the English boy and two Indian guides, from the Bermudas [Hundred, not Island], and came to his court or residence (as I judge, some three score miles distant from us, being seated at the head almost of Pamunkey River, at a town called Matchcot) the next night after, about twelve of the clock, the former night lodging in the open woods, fearless and without danger. When we were come opposite to his town, the main river between him and us, lest at any time we should march by land unto him undiscovered. My Indian guides called for a canoe (a boat made only of one tree, after the fashion of a hollow trough) to transport us, giving them to know that there was two English sent upon business to Powhatan from the English werowance.... Once known, a canoe was presently sent, and we ferried over, Powhatan himself attending at the landing place to welcome us. His first salutation was to the boy, whom he very well remembered, after this manner: "My child you are welcome. You have been a stranger to me these four years, at what time I gave you leave to go to Paspahegh"—for so was Jamestown called before our seating there—"to see your friends, and till now you never returned. You," said he, "are my child, by the donative of Captain Newport, in lieu of one of my subjects, Namontack, who I purposely sent to King James his land, to see him and his country, and to return me the true report thereof. He as yet is not returned, though many ships have arrived here from thence since that time. How ye have dealt with him, I know not." Having thus ended his speech to him, he addressed himself to me, and his first salutation, without any words at all, was about my neck, and with his hand he feeled round about it, so as I might have imagined he would have cut my throat, but that I knew he durst not. He asked me where the chain of pearl was; I demanded what chain. "That," said he, "which I sent my brother Sir Thomas Dale for a present, at his first arrival; which chain, since the peace concluded, he sent me word, if he sent any Englishman upon occasion of business to me, he should wear about his neck, otherwise I had order from him to bind him and send him home again." It is true Sir Thomas Dale had sent him such word (which till then myself never heard of), and for this purpose had given his page order to deliver me the said chain, who forgot it. I was doubtful at the first how to answer him, yet presently I replied that I was not ignorant of that message from his brother, formerly sent unto him, whereby he only intended that if upon extraordinary and sudden occasion, he should be constrained to send an Englishman unto him without an Indian guide, then in testimony that he sent him he should wear the chain about his neck. But, in case any of his own people should conduct any English unto him, as did me two of his own men, one of them a counselor unto him who was acquainted with my business, their testimony should be sufficient, and the chain then needeless to be worn. Which answer pleased him well, and forthwith he brought us to his house, not full a stone's cast from the waterside, whereinto being come, himself sat down on his bedstead side. Bed there was none more then a single mat, on each hand of him was placed a comely and personable young woman, not twenty years old the eldest, which they call his Queens. The house within round about be set with them, the outside guarded with a hundred bowmen, with their quivers of arrows at their backs, which at all times and places attend his person.

The first thing he offered us was a pipe of tobacco, which they called piffimore, whereof himself first drank, and then gave it to me, and when I had drank what I pleased, I returned his pipe, which with his own hands he vouchsafed to take from me. Then began he to inquire how his brother Sir Thomas Dale fared, after that of his daughter's welfare, her marriage, his unknown [grand-]son, and how they liked, lived and loved together. I resolved him that his brother was very well, and his daughter so well content that she would not change her life to return and live with him, whereat he laughed heartily, and said he was very glad of it. "Now proceed," said he, "to deliver the cause of your unexpected coming." I certified him my message was private, to be delivered to himself, without the presence of any, save one of his counselors, by name Pepaschicher, one of my guides, who was acquainted with my business. He instantly commanded all, both men and women, out of the house, his two Queens only excepted, who upon no occasion whatsoever may sequester themselves. "Now," said he, "speak on," and myself, by my interpreter, thus begun:

"Sir Thomas Dale your brother, the principal commander of the Englishmen, sends you greeting of love and peace, on his part inviolable, and hath in testimony thereof by me sent you a worthy present," viz, two large pieces of copper, five strings of white and blue beads, five wooden combs, ten fishhooks, and a pair of knives, all which I delivered him, one thing after another, that he might have time to view each particular. "He willed me also to certify you that when you pleased to send men, he would give you a great grinding stone." My message and gift hitherto pleased him; I proceeded thus. "The bruit of the exquisite perfection of your youngest daughter, being famous through all your territories, hath come to the hearing of your brother Sir Thomas Dale, who for this purpose hath addressed me hither, to entreat you by that brotherly friendship you make profession of, to permit her (with me) to return unto him, partly for the desire which himself hath, and partly for the desire her sister hath to see her of whom, if fame hath not been prodigal, as like enough it hath not, your brother (by your favor) would gladly make his nearest companion, wife, and bedfellow." Many times he would have interrupted my speech, which I entreated him to hear out, and then if he pleased to return me answer. "And the reason hereof is, because being now friendly and firmly united together, and made one people (as he supposeth and believes) in the band of love, he would make a natural union between us, principally because himself hath taken resolution to dwell in your country so long as he liveth, and would therefore not only have the firmest assurance he may of perpetual friendship from you, but also hereby bind himself thereunto."

When I had thus made an end of speaking, the sooner by his often interruption, I had no need to require his answer, which readily, and with no less gravity, he returned thus:

"I gladly accept your King's salute of love and peace, which while I live I shall exactly, both myself and subjects, maintain and conserve. His pledges thereof I receive with no less thanks, albeit they are not so ample, howbeit himself a greater werowance, as formerly Captain Newport, whom I very well love, was accustomed to gratify me with. But to the purpose—my daughter whom my brother desireth, I sold within a these few days to be wife to a great werowance for two bushels of roanoke (a small kind of beads made of oyster shells, which they use and pass one to another as we do money, a cubit's length valuing six pence), and it is true she is already gone with him, three days' journey from me."

I replied that I knew his greatness and power to be such that if he pleased herein to gratify his brother he might, restoring the roanoke without the imputation of injustice, take home his daughter again, the rather because she was not full twelve years old, and therefore not marriageable; assuring him beside the band of peace so much the firmer, he should have treble the price of his daughter, in beads, copper, hatchets, and many other things more useful for him. His answer hereunto was that he loved his daughter as dear as his own life, and though he had many children, he delighted in none so much as in her, whom if he should not often behold, he could not possibly live, which she living with us he knew he could not, having with himself resolved upon no terms whatsoever to put himself into our hands, or come amongst us, and therefore entreated me to urge that suit no further, but return his brother this answer:

"I desire no firmer assurance of his friendship than his promise which he hath already made unto me. From me, he hath a pledge, one of my daughters, which so long as she lives shall be sufficient; when she dieth, he shall have another child of mine, but she yet liveth. I hold it not a brotherly part of your king to desire to bereave me of two of my children at once. Further give him to understand that if he had no pledge at all he should not need to distrust any injury from me, or any under my subjection. There have been too many of his and my men killed, and by my occasion there shall never be more. I, which have power to perform it, have said it. No, not though I should have just occasion offered, for I am now old, and would gladly end my days in peace, so as if the English offer me injury, my country is large enough, I will remove myself farther from you. Thus much I hope will satisfy my brother. Now because yourselves are weary, and I sleepy, we will thus end the discourse of this business."

Then called he one of his men, and willed him to get some bread for us, himself the meanwhile telling us that they not expected our coming, as usually they do eat up all their other victuals. Presently the bread was brought in two great wooden bowls . . . whereof we eat some few, and disposed the rest to many of his hungry guard which attended about us. When we had eaten he caused to be fetched a great glass of sack, some three quarts or better, which Captain Newport had given him six or seven years since, carefully preserved by him, not much above a pint in all this time spent, and gave each of us in a great oyster shell some three spoonfulls. And so, giving order to one of his people to appoint us a house to lodge in, took his leave for that night, and we departed. We had not been half an hour in the house before the fleas began so to torment us that we could not rest there, but went forth, and under a broad oak, upon a mat, reposed ourselves that night. No sooner were we awaked and up in the morning, but Powhatan himself came to us, and asked us how we fared, and immediately led us to his house, where was provided for our breakfast a great bowl of Indian peas and beans boiled together, and as much bread as might have sufficed a dozen hungry men; about an hour after, boiled fresh fish, and not long after that, roasted oysters, crevices, and crabs. His men in this time being abroad a-hunting some venison, others turkeys and such like beasts and fowls as their woods afford, who returned before ten of the clock with three does and a buck, very good and fat venison, and two great cock turkeys, all which were dressed that day, and supper ended, scarce a bone to be seen.

While I yet remained there, by great chance came an Englishman thither, almost three years before that time surprised as he was at work near Fort Henry: one William Parker, grown so like both in complexion and habit to the Indians that I only knew him by his tongue to be an Englishman. He seemed very joyful, so happily to meet me there. Of him when we often inquired, the Indians ever told us that he fell sick and died, which till now we believed. He entreated me to use my best endeavors to procure his return, which thing I was purposed so soon as I knew him, and immediately went with him to Powhatan, and told him that we credibly believed that he was dead, but since it was otherwise I must needs have him home, for myself of necessity must acquaint his brother that I had seen him there; who, if he returned not, would make another voyage thither purposely for him. Powhatan seemed very much discontent, and thus replied, "You have one of my daughters with you, and I am therewith well content, but you can no sooner see or know of any Englishman's being with me, but you must have him away, or else break peace and friendship. If you must needs have him, he shall go with you, but I will send no guides along with you, so as if any ill befall you by the way, thank yourselves."

I answered that rather than I would go without him, I would go alone; the way I knew well enough, and other dangers I feared not, since if I returned not safely, he must expect our revenge upon him and his people, giving him further to know, that his brother our king might have just occasion to distrust his love to him by his slight respect of me, if he returned me home without guides. He replied not hereunto, but in passion and discontentment from me, not till suppertime speaking any more unto me. When sending for me, he gave me share of such cakes as were for himself provided, and as good aspect and countenance as before, but not a word concerning my return, till himself at midnight coming to me and the boy where we lay, awaked us, and told me that Pepaschicher and another of his men in the morning should accompany us home, earnestly requesting me to remember his brother to send him these particulars: ten pieces of copper; a shaving knife; an iron frow to cleave boards; a grinding stone, not so big but four or five men may carry it, which would be big enough for his use; two bone combs such as Captain Newport had given him—the wooden ones his own men can make; a hundred fishhooks, or, if he could spare it, rather a fishing seine; and a cat, and a dog, with which things if his brother would furnish him, he would requite his love with the return of skins, wherewith he was now altogether unfurnished (as he told me), which yet I knew he was well stored with, but his disposition, mistrustful and jealous, loves to be on the surer hand.

When he had delivered this his message, he asked me if I will remember every particular, which I must repeat to him for his assurance, and yet still doubtful that I might forget any of them, he bade me write them down in such a table book as he showed me, which was a very fair one. I desired him, it being of no use to him, to give it me, but he told me it did him much good to show it to strangers which came unto him. So in mine own table book I wrote down each particular, and he departed.

In the morning, himself and we were timely stirring to be gone. To breakfast first we went, with a good boiled turkey, which ended, he gave us a whole turkey, besides that we left, and three baskets of bread to carry us home. And when we were ready to depart, he gave each of us an excellent buckskin, very well dressed and white as snow, and sent his son and daughter each of them one, demanding if I well remembered his answer to his brother, which I repeated to him. "I hope," said he, "this will give him good satisfaction; if it do not, I will go three days' journey farther from him, and never see Englishman more. If upon any other occasion he sent to me again, I will gladly entertain his messengers and, to my power, accomplish his just requests." And even thus himself conducting us to the water side, he took leave of us, and we of him. . . .

NOTES

1. Hamor, Ralph, *A True Discourse of the Present Estate of Virginia* (London: Printed at London by John Beale for William Welby, dwelling at the sign of the Swanne in Paul's church yard, 1615), 37-46.

2. Hume, Ivor Noel, *The Virginia Adventure: Roanoke to James Towne, An Archaeological and Historical Odyssey* (Charlottesville: University Press of Virginia, 1994), 332.

3. Several accounts refer to Pocahontas as Powhatan's only daughter.

Bibliography

Brown, Alexander. *Genesis of the United States*. Cambridge: The Riverside Press, 1890.

Chapman, George, Ben Jonson, and John Marston. *Eastward Hoe*, edited with an introduction, glossary and notes by Julia Hamlet Harris. New Haven: Yale University Press, 1926.

Force, Peter. *Tracts and Other Papers Relating Principally to the origin, settlement, and progress of the colonies in North America, from the Discovery of the country to the year 1776*. Washington: Printed by Peter Force, 1836-46.

Hamor, Ralph. *A True Discourse of the Present Estate of Virginia* . . . London: Printed at London by John Beale for William Welby, dwelling at the sign of the Swanne in Paul's church yard, 1615.

Hume, Ivor Noel. *The Virginia Adventure: Roanoke to James Towne, An Archaeological and Historical Odyssey*.

Charlottesville: University Press of Virginia, 1994.

Kermode, Frank. *Shakespeare's Language*. New York: Penguin Books, 2001.

Kupperman, Karen Ordahl. *Captain John Smith: A Select Edition of His Writings*. Chapel Hill: University of North Carolina Press, 1988.

Miller, Lee. *Roanoke: Solving the Mystery of the Lost Colony*. New York: Arcade Publishing, 2001.

Neill, Edward D. *History of the Virginia Company of London*. Albany: Joel Munsell, 1869.

Nova Britannia: Offering Most Excellen fruits by Planting in Virginia, Exciting all such as be well affected to further the same. London, 1609.

Palmer, Alan and Veronica. *Who's Who in Shakespeare's England*. New York: St. Martin's Press, 1999.

Percy, George. "A Trewe Relacyon." Richmond: *Tyler's Quarterly Historical and Genealogical Magazine*, Volume III, no. 2, 1922.

Purchas, Samuel. *Haklutus Posthumus, or Purchas his Pilgrimes*. London: Imprinted for Henry Fetherston at the sign of the rose in Paul's church yard, 1625.

Rountree, Helen C. *The Powhatan Indians of Virginia*. Norman: University of Oklahoma Press, 1989.

Rubin, Louis D. *Virginia: A Bicentennial History*. New York: W. W. Norton & Company, 1977.

Smith, John. *The General History of Virginia, New England, and the Summer Isles*. London: Printed by I.D. and I.H. for Michael Sparkes, 1624.

Smith, John. *A True Relation of Virginia*, edited with an introduction and notes by Charles Deane. Boston: Wiggin and Lunt, 1866.

Spelman, Henry. *Relation of Virginia*. 1609. London: Printed for